Bitter Chocolate

Also by Toyin Adewale-Gabriel:
Naked Testimonies

Bitter Chocolate

STORIES

Toyin Adewale-Gabriel

MALLORY PUBLISHING

Published by
Mallory Publishing,
Aylesbeare Common Business Park,
Exmouth Road,
Aylesbeare,
Devon,
EX5 2DG,
England

For a complete list of titles, visit
http://www.mallorypublishing.co.uk
e-mail: admin@mallorypublishing.co.uk

First published 2010 by Mallory Publishing
Copyright © Toyin Adewale-Gabriel 2010

ISBN 978 1 85657 110 4

Cover design © Mallory International Limited 2006,
2010

For Tayelolu Adebola

Omo gidi, Omo ayiye
Beloved brother, calm centre, heart's cry

Mallory New African Writing
An Introduction

New African Writing was launched in 2006, in conjunction with an initiative by the British Council, and featured unpublished works by promising African writers, some of them previously unpublished. I need to record our thanks to Richard Weyers, Director of the British Council in Uganda at the time. *New African Writing* was his idea, and I think it is the kind of initiative which shows the British Council at its best.

Mallory International is primarily a bookseller, and most of our business is in Africa, so we have a commitment to African education and culture, and publishing gives us an opportunity both to publish new works and (through our *Classic African Writing* series) to improve the availability of past African classics which have been allowed to go out of print. We have previously re-published Toyin Adewale Gabriel's poetry, and were very pleased to have the opportunity to issue this brilliant collection of short stories.

Julian Hardinge

Contents

Bitter Chocolate

It is lonely at this end of the world. The dust on the floor is quiet. It is submissive. The grains of sand lie prostrate. No wind stirs them up. You etch your days on the sand. I have been here for eight months. You say to yourself. Two hundred and thirty-eight lines glare back at you from the dust. A line for each day.

You scratch your thigh, trying hard to reach the reachable itch. If you had a pair of scissors, you would probe deep into your flesh after the itch. You would chase it along the highways of your blood stream and draw it out but there is no scissors. There is nothing sharp around here. They have taken everything away. Your jailers. You scratch, parting your thighs, bending them like two Vs facing each other. Your skin flakes onto your hand. Your once–lovely–ebony–smooth–craftman–polished skin. Your glowing skin, so alight it struck a man's eyes and he could not see any other woman but you. And he had to marry you to regain his sight.

Skin rashes fester all over your body. Where the bed bugs and cockroaches left off after the night, the germs continued by day. They gave you no soap for your bath since the last one your husband brought finished. You asked the doctor to get you a tube of Troysd cream to cure the rashes on you. He said 'I cannot promise. I will look into the stock we have and if there is one, I will make sure you get it.' And if there is none, would your skin perish in the dust? He avoids your eyes and makes no answer. He shuffles out of the room.

The unreachable itch, you keep at it. All your fingernails are broken but at least it helps to while away the silence. This eternity of time you do not want. And there was evening and there was morning, the fourth day, and there was evening and there was morning, the sixth month. And time flows on, leaving you gasping for breath, desperately etching your days in the dust.

You keep scratching your thighs. Your woman smell pervades your nostrils. Your panties unwashed for three days, redolent with dried piss and all your juices. You are in the middle of your body cycle. Your egg–white juice flows into crystal clear elastic liquid. It stretches and stretches. You could almost lay it from one end of the room to the other. In another time, in another place, it would have been a season to hug your husband, to squeeze him deep in you, holding him tight with all your woman muscles and he would sigh and come and cry a little, flooding you with his seed, gazing at you from behind his love eyes.

This four-by-four cul de sac with a little about-to-die light bulb and a window which threw in a tiny shaft of light. A window way high beyond your highest reach, an armed window, riddled with steel bars that had nail teeth. A piss pot stood in the corner and beside your cot, a little stack of books. The books keep your mind alive but they do not answer your hunger. Your thirst for news. This is your greatest pain. The starvation diet of no news. The news is breaking all round the world. Flash bulbs are exploding. CNN is bursting loose but the news spills without you. Students riot in Indonesia. Hundreds are dead. Fuel crisis paralyses Lagos. Leaders betray acolytes, sentencing them to the firing squad. Sycophants import rice for kings who would never leave their thrones even for their sons' sons but you do not know all of this.

Once a month, they allow your husband to speak to you across a steel barricade for thirty minutes. He holds up new photos of your daughter and her scrawled multi-crayoned greeting, "l love you Mummy, when are you coming home?"

You say to him, "what is news?"

He tells you, "The courtiers have said the king must stay on. The royal cobbler says his leather, nails and hammer were custom made in Italy for the king. No one else can wear his shoes. The royal chef says his recipes are crafted solely for the king's pleasure. Everyday, praise singers hold concerts in the place courtyard shouting his praise, saying he is the only lord who can rule the land. His servants have threatened mass suicide if he leaves the throne. Day by day, the royal drums announce the visits of hungry delegations who have crossed the deserts and the seas just to beg the king not to leave the throne."

You say to him in rising anger, "But the law of the land says the king must leave after ruling for four years!"

Your husband says to you, "there is no law in this land. A royal decree has been promulgated saying the king can rule for all eternity if the people so wishes and delegations of chiefs all across the land are falling at the king's feet begging him in the name of the people to please stay on…"

You ask your husband, "And the king, what does he say?" "He gives them some bags of rice and bars of soap and says nothing"

"He says nothing?"

"Yes, he says nothing…"

A prison warder comes in and taps your husband on the shoulder. "Time up" he barks….

Your husband hands to the warder a plastic bag containing four bars of medicated soap, three cartons of fruit juice, some biscuits, a jar of body cream, a little tub of butter, two packets of sugar, two tins of Ovaltine Cocoa beverage and some money. You know you will only get half of it, the prison warder will steal the other half and take it home to his family as booty.

Your husband stands from the stool he has been sitting on and walks out backwards, keeping you within his still love struck eyes and blowing you kisses as he melts out of sight. Your daughter's question looms before you: "Mummy, when are you coming home?"

"…I don't know honey, I don't know." In your anger, you want to curse the warder's children. You know they are out under the trees playing with their own mother while your daughter is curled up in front of a television set, comforting herself with kiddies cartoons until daddy comes back from visiting mummy in prison. Curses begin to bubble from your mouth. They float vigorously, forming a circle, traveling towards the prison warder: may his children become orphaned… may an east wind blight his harvest, may he sow a hundred – fold and reap emptiness. The curses begins to close in on him. Closer. Closer. But you draw them back, you break up the circle of curses and burn them in a heap of fire. Why orphan his children with curses when the guardians of the nation have mortgaged the lives of the people for bags of rice and bars of soap? Why soak the bloodied land with more blood?

As the warder opens the door of the little cubicle to lead you back to your cell, you know the plastic bag is already lighter. He has stolen your property in a picosecond. He hands over the bag to you. His hand lingers on your hand, his thumb caresses your palm. You snarl at him and hurry your footsteps into your cell. The door clangs shut. You sit on your cot and tear open with your teeth, a pack of biscuits and a carton of orange juice. You laugh softly to yourself, as you begin to munch, at how redundant knives, spoons, plate and cups can be when a woman has the full gift of thirty–two sharp teeth in her mouth.

Between the fourth and fifth chocolate coated biscuit, your husband has smuggled a note. You open it and read, "I love you very much. I wish I could take you in my arms right now. It's really hard on me at night…."

The sinews of fear grapple for a stranglehold on your heart. What is he trying to say to you? You try to unravel his words because you know the powers of words. You do business with words. It was your words that got you into jail. Your screaming cover story that sold out your weekly news magazine in one day – KING BREAKS HIS PROMISE. HE SHALL NOT LEAVE ON THE 12TH OF JUNE!

You had heard rumours of a plot orchestrated by the king to ensure his eternity in power. The news hound you are tracked the reports, traveling round the country, researching reliable sources and conducting interviews with palace aides who were willing to talk in anonymity. And then you crafted the story in prose worthy of the Pulitzer prize. The news hit the four winds. The winds ran with the news like motorcycle outriders to the center and outposts of the country. The people were dazed. The king they hailed as a patriot and a genuine lover of the people had promised them in a lyrical moment —"I do not need riots to make me leave. I shall leave on the 12th of June and hand over to a democratically elected government".

Your carefully researched story had spilled the state secret and his hounds had come calling. They hauled you before a court hastily convened at night. The bleary eyed judge dressed in judicial wig and his bedroom slippers kept dozing off through the court proceedings. He woke up in time to sentence you to twenty five years imprisonment for intent to cause a revolt against the king.....

And eight months into twenty five years, you are chewing your husband's words: "It's really hard on me at night", your daughter's "mummy, when are you coming home?"

The bitter words are crunching in the chocolate biscuits under your molars. Bitter chocolate. What is your husband saying to you? Who has he started sleeping with? Will his love struck eyes last the years in the distance? Will your daughter love another mummy? You chew your biscuits. You gulp the orange juice in the carton. You cling to the present. Who knows? Perhaps today, they will walk you into the final night at three in the afternoon.

Wig in the Morning

"It was at the Oba's market, the market where my cousin owns a shop. I was bending over a bale of second hand clothing, looking for suitable T-shirts for my daughter, Shade. While sorting though the clothes, I saw a lawyer's wig. A mass of tightly woven white curls. It was the wig I saw in my dream."

"Ha, it really seems significant, a lawyer's wig in a bale of second hand clothing…."

"I am really afraid. In that dream, I abandoned my search for T-shirts. I bought the wig, and wrapped it up neatly. I intended to give it to Lawyer Kunle as soon as I got home. I began to walk to the market, pushing my way through the crowd, when suddenly, my limbs grew heavy. I could not run, I felt like l had the body of an elephant and the legs of a cockroach. I crumbled on my knees. Something glued me to the spot and began to suck me backwards.

I was sucked into a red room, every space in it was painted blood red, the walls, the ceiling, the floor."

"You are making me worried. It is a strange dream. Do you often have nightmares like this?"

"No, that is why I am taking this seriously. In the red room, I saw a white skull, completely bleached of all flesh, laughing and howling over two dead bodies on the floor. Both corpses were males, dressed in lawyers' gowns except that one of the corpses had no wig on."

"The skull ordered me to unwrap the wig in my hands and place it on the head of the wigless corpse. I unwrapped the wig and tremblingly moved close to the wigless corpse. As I moved closer, I got a good look at the corpse. It was Lawyer Kunle. I dropped the wig and started screaming. My husband shook me awake, he said I was screaming loud enough to wake the whole house. I told him about the dream."

"What did he say?"

"He patted me on the back and said my imagination was too wild. He turned on his side and went back to sleep."

"I hope he will be safe. I hope they will spare him this time. He was almost killed the last time they took him away. They came for him in the middle of the night and drove him to the outskirts of Lagos. They beat him thoroughly and left him to the mercy of snakes in the forest. He kept wandering around, trying to find his way out, not knowing he was getting deeper and deeper into the bush. A hunter saw him and mistook him for a baboon. He aimed at him and nearly shot him. He said he cried to the hunter, 'I am a human being, don't shoot me.'"

"The hunter kindly led him out of the forest and gave money to return home."

"I hope he will be lucky this time. Your dream really frightens me. A lawyer's wig in a heap of second hand clothing... Lawyers' wigs are very expensive. You will never find them so casually discarded in real life. The red room and the skull. Your dream scares me... It reeks so much of death. I hope he will be alright. His children are too young to be orphaned. His oldest is only seven."

"I hear they came for him four days ago. We went to an overnight party at Imeko. We returned and met the whole street buzzing with the news. I hear the noise woke up everyone."

"My dear, it was quite dreadful. They pounded on the gate of their house like a bunch of irresponsible drunks. The noise woke me up. At first, I thought they were thieves, come to rob us. I was scared stiff. I carefully got out of bed, making sure that the bedsprings did not creak. I tiptoed to my dressing table, reached for the touchlight and cautiously drew my window drapes before switching on the touch light.

Piece by piece, I began to hide my gold jewelry and most of the hundred thousand naira I had in the house, in different hiding places...in old shoes, in the hole in the ceiling, wherever came to my mind."

"Ha, ha, ha.... Ha, ha, ha...."

"Now it sounds funny. I was so scared. I was almost shitting in my pants. I didn't dare go to the toilet because it had a very creaky door. I couldn't afford any noise. I kept twenty thousand naira in my bag as an "offering" for the thieves in case they came to my apartment. You know sometimes, they can angrily kill if the victim is empty-handed. I re-checked the bolt on my bedroom door and crawled under the bed."

"The racket was still going on. They kept pounding on the gate. Then l heard Lawyer Kunle's wife voice."

"You heard her voice?"

"I did, she is a very strong woman. She was shouting boldly, ' I will not open the gate'. I heard a man say, 'Madam Kunle!, open this gate, or else I will break it down. Your landlord won't be happy with that, will he? He will make you pay for the repairs and make you quit. You know good houses are difficult to find in Lagos. Where will you get another house? Open this gate in your best interest.'

"Did she open the gate?"

"No, I tell you, the woman is very strong. When I heard the exchange. I crawled out of hiding and pulled back the drapes. I looked out of the window and saw a light blue Peugeot station-wagon car, parked outside the gate."

"One man was lounging on the car, smoking a cigarette. Two men were banging on the gate. I couldn't see their faces. It was dark but they appeared lean and tall."

"So three men came for him?"

"Yes. I heard his wife shout again, 'I will not open the gate until seven a.m. Then the whole street will be awake. I want everyone to see you'. One of the men said 'woman, open this gate, your husband is a lawyer, he knows the consequences of resisting arrest' she shouted back 'I have told you, I will not open this gate, do whatever you like.'"

"She said that to the secret service men?"

"She sure did. I heard it all. Everyone on the street could hear her. The man, now exasperated, said, 'You want me to wait here until seven a.m. You want me to wait two more hours. All right, I will wait, but don't blame me for the consequences.'

"Mrs. Kunle did not give him any further reply. The men began muttering among themselves. They all lit cigarettes and began to smoke. Silence reigned for a while but suddenly, the heavens opened and a heavy rain began."

"The men must have driven away..."

"You don't know how tenacious they can be. They simply took refuge inside the car, wound up the windows and waited until the rain stopped..."

"They must have wanted him badly, to sit through nearly two hours of heavy rain."

"When the rain started, I went back to bed and crept under the blankets, wondering what we could all do to help this neighbour in distress. The rain dwindled to a trickle before seven a.m. At about ten minutes to seven, an early morning caller came knocking, asking to see Mrs. Kunle. I quickly climbed out of bed and resumed watch behind the curtain drapes. Mrs. Kunle came out of the house with her baby wrapped on her back. She held her older child by the hand. She greeted her caller, opened the gate and began to talk to the secret service men, 'I hope you had a nice, long wait. You guys are all young men, you're supposed to be gentlemen. Yet, you rudely come to bang my gate in the middle of the night, walking up my kids and all the neighbours. Show me your search warrants'"

"Did they have the search warrants?"

"Well, they drew some papers out of their pockets and showed them to her. She looked at the papers and said they were not genuine. She reminded them of how you came some weeks ago, saying he was wanted for a friendly chat at their headquarters. 'I allowed him to go but you kidnapped him. You beat him up and nearly killed him in the forest. I will not let you take away my husband like that...'"

"They just shoved her aside and went inside the house. Then I saw Mrs. Kunle whispering quickly to her caller and running with her children and her friend into her friend's car. They drove off quickly."

"So she let the secret servicemen take away her husband after all.."

"No, her husband was not in the house at all. All the shouting she had done were diversion tactics to give him time to escape. The men searched their home for nearly one hour and left with a bundle of papers. Mrs. Kunle came back about one hour after they had left with some of her husband's family members and friends.

"Have you seen her husband since then?"

"No, I think he is still hiding…"

"I hope he will be all right,"

"I hope so too. Please don't tell her your dream."

"I wouldn't dare."

Cascades

Hurtling, hurtling, hurtling down the road, the rain picks up speed. The rain is insolent. It has the wind in its grip. Behold a jealous rain, it will not let go. The papers try to scamper for cover. The dust has no hideout. All is beaten, all is trampled.

Ka, ka, ka, ka, the tin roofs are dancing in the wind. The serrated edges are having a conga dance, lifting up their skirts from the roofs, right up....

And London bridge is falling down. Hey, hey, I've got a hungry woman in my house. London bridge is falling down, my fair lady! In the corridors of the mind, the nursery rhyme battles the cobwebs, springing out with lucid steps. It is the song of crisis, for a very bad day. He hopes he is not going crazy.

Inside, in the bedroom, she stands on the threshold of life. She is the gateway. Like a doll figurine. She has got a bell inside. It is ringing inside her. She is swimming in pain. She is wallowing in hunger, woman of the empty kitchen and the jobless husband. She is several hours hungry. She has got a baby in her womb. She cannot put her swollen breasts to her mouth and suck. Where is the Lord God of Elijah who bears bread and water in the wilderness?

The rain is still falling hard, cloaking the windows like a starched cotton bed sheet ironed with spit and zeal. Her kitchen bin gives up nothing eatable. The air speaks terrifyingly. Dear disturbed man. Dear hungry woman and a landscape desolate of miracles.

Tunji enters the bedroom, with trembling hands, he lifts her into his arms.

"Sweetheart, let me run down to the Adamus. I think they might be able to give us some food. The rain is not stopping. Please drink a little water. Maybe it will reduce the hunger."

He is crying on the inside as she drinks the water. Her stomach moves to the tune of want. His flesh is cut to the bone.

Was this the elephant tusks he promised for the feet of this beautiful woman carrying his daughter? The gale sighs in the room. He lifts the cup from her hands and lays her back gently on the bed. He sits on the edge of the bed and removes his tired shoes. His blackened toe nails peep out from torn smelly socks. The rotten fishy smell pervades the air.

The Kosoko Railway Corporation was in trouble again. He and his colleagues had not been paid for the past six months. Their families were all in beggared situations. Most had farmed out their children to family and friends, who were using them as cheap sources of labour. They washed clothes, ironed and slaved for these benefactors who in turn gave them room and board.

Their landlords had given most of them quit notices to worry about. As Tunji's landlord told him,

"Look, my friend, I pity you but I am not the government. I have a lot of responsibilities. My eldest son has just gained admission to the law school. I have two young daughters in university. I also have a lot of bills. You must move out."

Slyly, he quoted the proverb of self survival – "if one is caught in a fire with one's child, one must first of all douse the fire on oneself before the child can be helped."

Tunji and his colleagues protested and cried to the government to no avail. They were only told that government had no funds and 'government would look into it and do something as soon as funds were available'.

What had happened to all the money made from the railways? All around the country, the trains were lying down like dead rats in the streets. The rail lines were weeping for maintenance. Some of the rail tracks passing through major cities were barely recognizable. They had not been replaced since independence. They had sank in puddles of stagnant water where railway markets had sprung up. The market women balanced their goods and their mobile stools like acrobats walking the tight rope. Passers by learned to walk gingerly, taking great care not to slip on banana and orange peels. There were no new trains and railway staff were condemned to wearing thread bare uniforms beneath their dignity. But first, human beings must eat to live.

Her salary had fed them most of the time, a mere inadequate pittance. There were baby's things to be bought and hospital bills to settle. And now she was on maternity leave, her pay had been cut by half by the power of company rules which stated that a woman on three months maternity leave could only collect a half salary. They had borrowed and borrowed until there was no where else to turn.

The rain is slowing down. She gives him a weak smile as he bends to pull on his shoes. He looks at her. He does not want to leave her alone in the house. He is too afraid....

From the window of her flat across the road, Yetunde looks out. Her walkman is plugged into her ears. She is glad that the weather is clearing. She is whistling under her breath as she cuts the pieces of yam into cubes. Soon Dapo will be back from work. Her movements are eager like that of a woman in want. It will be a good evening to commune with their bodies. The weather was just right for snuggling in bed. She is smiling to herself trying to guess what present her husband would bring her. He always brought her a gift every pay day.

She takes a look around her kitchen. Her kitchen larders are all yawning. She is grateful that today is Dapo's pay day. They desperately needed to shop for food. She takes the second half of yam. As she is about to peel, someone behind her says "Take the other half to the Adebayos' across the road."

"Dapo, don't frighten me. When did you......"

She turns to leap into her husband's arms. She encounters the empty air. There is nobody else in the kitchen. Oh, oh, who spoke to her? The vice of fear grips her heart, she feels invaded. Panicky, she races to every room in the house, standing back to fling the doors open, ready to fly like the wind. She finds no one.

As she picks up her walkman from where it had fallen, the voice comes again,

"Yetunde, take down the yam. She is hungry."

She is scared. She knows there is no one else in the house. Like a drop of stone rippling in the water, it slowly dawns on her that perhaps God might be talking to her. She heard the preacher say in Church that God still speaks to people. Then she had dismissed it as a whole lot of pentecostal rubbish completely out of step with the technicolor age of genetic cloning. She thought the preachers were employing marketing strategies, promising the voice of God as a benefit to whoever became a member of their church.

What was happening to her? Tentatively, she tries to speak.

"Who are you. Why are you speaking to me? Surely, you know Dapo has a huge appetite.

He will come home very hungry, how can I spare a whole half of this little tuber of yam? They say charity begins at home, you know."

Suddenly, the sunday school story she had heard as a little girl floods her mind, the story of a widow in a town called Zapareth, a woman like her, called to make a move into the future provision that she could not see. A woman who decided to share the little flour and oil she had.

"O well, it's a dry piece of yam. They say dry pieces of yam can really swell in the pot and be very filling. I expect this other half will feed us to night. ….But, but, we do not even greet each other.

How can I just walk up to them and give them a piece of yam. What are you trying to get me into, they might even slap me. They will most likely feel insulted. They haven't come begging for food, you know."

She marshals her arguments against sharing her precious tuber of yam but her excuses bounce back at her from the wall. From within her belly, something strong urges her to go.

"Alright, Alright………"

Deftly, she wraps the yam in a piece of newspaper and puts it in a black carrier bag. She races across the road and walks into the house where the Adebayos live. The corridor is dark even though it is bright noon outside. There are half-naked kids racing, playing up and down the corridor. Their protruding bellies are glistening. She stops one of the children and asks for the Adebayos door.

The child points at a door with a torn curtain overhanging it. She knocks once, then twice. She is about to knock a third time, her courage melts into the gloomy corridor. Yetunde hangs the black carrier bag on the door handle and flees.

Tunji is wearing his left shoe when he hears the knocks on the door. He hopes whoever is there will not detain him.... he walks to the door, turns the lock and opens the door. A black carrier bag falls on the ground. He rotates three hundred and sixty degrees on the earth's axis. What new enemies had they made? He thought he had only hunger to battle. Why would anyone leave a black carrier bag at his door? He dies a little; he dashes into the house and brings out a long stick. He starts thrashing the bag from a calculated distance. There are no explosions. The bag tears apart, revealing bits of newspaper and a slightly bruised piece of yam. Tunji races to the yam and falls onto his knees.

Tunji tenderly lifts the yam. He gently removes the layers of paper. He can hear a new rhythm on the wind. He can smell the soil fresh from a rain bath. A sun ray penetrates the dark corridor, it caress his face. He knows the sonorous drums are asking for a dance. He breaks loose.

Rice Hips

She is chewing soft, warm bread with chunks of coconut flesh and, thinking how good it is to sit under the shade of coconut palms. She feels the sun piercing needle-like through the roof of the shelter. She hears the faint voices of children playing in front of the fishermen's huts. She is alone and it feels good.

Behind her sunglasses, she gazes out at a sky clear of clouds. The Atlantic ocean is kissing the sand at her feet, she knows that tiny crabs are crawling all over the sand. All round her, sea life is breathing. Fishes are being hatched, fishes are being eaten. The fishermen are hunting the sea with much hope.

But all these are not really on her mind. She is just lazing in the sun, spending time with herself on this long and narrow beach, nestling tiny fishermen's villages. All around her, ripe coconuts are falling, thud, thud on crystal sand. More than one hour away from the city and not yet discovered by tourists, the beach was often deserted for long stretches of sand. So she could easily take walks, picking up gifts of quiet, like shells in the sand. She is a reveler in the cold fragrance of the sea and wet fish.

The excited voice of a child breaks into her daydreams:

"Auntie Sola, Uncle Lucky says you should come. Quick, hurry, the fishermen have arrived and they are already emptying their nets…"

She jumps to her feet and races with the child to the fishermen. Her friend Lucky, a fishermen is smiling. The catch must have been very good. She met Lucky a year ago when she first visited the beach. He was painstakingly repairing his wounded boat and she fell into conversation with him while watching him at work with deep fascination.

The sea's heaving waters have always attracted her, even though her friendship with it was strangely paradoxical. It calls to her but she will never ever swim in it. She likes to eat its fish but she cannot fish. She loves the sea but does not trust it. And when the tides turn and the waves grow angry and the breeze turns cold, she calmly picks her beach bag and heads home without a back ward glance....

Over the course of several visits, she became very good friends with Lucky and he would tell her stories about life at sea. Born on a coastal village in Ghana, he had come to Nigeria as a roving fisherman and had decided to live on the shores of the beach... Sometimes, he gave her gifts of fish.

"De fisherman don come, I say make de pickin go call you. E be like say today fish good well, well."

She stands beside him, caught in the tense excitement. The fishermen's wives were chattering in a small group holding large baskets in their hands. They watched the rippling muscles of the men glistening with sweat as they dragged in the nets. The nets were filled with wriggling fish and some octopuses. They began to sort the fish into varying sizes. The tension slowly loosened and she begins to walk back to her coconut fronds shelter with Lucky.

Suddenly she catches the strong smell of petrol in the air. She looks to her right, towards the fishermen's huts, wondering where the smell could be coming from. There were no petrol stations for miles around and the fishermen used canoes paddled by oars, not motor engines. She turns to Lucky.

"You no smell de petrol? Who dey carry petrol near here?"

"Na de water. Make you look de water."

She turns her eyes to the left and looks at the sea. There are several cans of big black jerrycans floating on the waves. Some men are swimming after them and trying to load them into six bobbing canoes. It looked like very slippery work from her distance.

"Wetin dem dey do with de jerry cans?"

"Dem dey carry petrol from Nigeria go Republic of Benin an odder places."

She felt like she had walked into the climax of a thriller story... were the customs officers aware of this? She says to Lucky:

"Customs no dey catch dem?"

"My sister, na wa. You know say dis una country, na so so wayo. Dem dey settle custom people but sometimes, custom dey catch dem!

"How dem manage now?"

"Dem dey carry petrol inside jerry can as you don see so. Dem go load am for canoe, come carry am go another boat for high sea." Sometimes, their canoe go turn like dis one... When night reach, dem go carry de big boat, begin go Republic of Benin with de petrol. If Navy police jam dem, dem go fight. Plenty of dem don die like that. De last one wey dem go, out of ten people, only six come back."

They reach her shelter and she begins to pick her things.

"You dey go?"

"I dey go... de petrol smell don spoil my belle."

The spectacle of lavish petrol smuggling in board daylight on this deserted beach in an oil rich country where petrol shortages at public fuel stations was fast becoming a tradition consumes her with anger. She burns, remembering the long treks the people of Lagos had to endure when there were fuel shortages, the exorbitant hike in transport fares....

Besides, these smugglers were ruining her treasured hide out, polluting the sea with oil slicks, staining the sea breeze with their crude trade. She walks dejectedly to the bus stop and takes a bus headed for the city center. On the bus, she seats in a tight squeeze between two women with very large hips. As the bus driver swerves to avoid the potholes on the road, their hips collide, grinding her hipbones in between. The bus is tightly packed with human beings, bags of rice and bales of second hand clothing, smuggled across the Seme border. The passengers feet, heavily laden with the dust of different journeys, can only find room on the bags of polished Thailand rice.

She switches her mind off thoughts of how they must be polluting the rice, she swishes away the images of bacteria and food poisoning looming before her... Every few minutes, the bus jerks to a halt before the customs and immigration official and unofficial road blocks. The driver stops because it is the wise option. The road blocks are built with twin drums sealed with concrete and planks of vicious looking nails. At each stop, a uniformed customs official peeps through the bus windows at the passengers. He pretends not to see the bags of smuggled rice.

The woman sitting on her left has a small bag propped up on her laps and this always drew attention from the customsmen.

"Madam, wetin you carry for leg?"

And she would reply, her voice laden with much suffering and hardwork, as if she had been abandoned to raise ten children all by heself, she would reply plaintively:

"Na small rice for my pickin."

Everyone was moved by her voice and no customs officer dared take the bag from her because he would have been immediately branded as an heartless man who wanted to starve a poor woman and her children. Everyone in the bus would have pleaded for her with one voice:

"Oga make you leave de woman now, Na food for her pickun. Haba, sebi na woman born you too......."

On hearing her "Na small rice for my pickin...." the customs officer would walk away, patrol slowly round the bus and end his journey at the driver's side to collect his 'settlement'. Like a snake slithering in the grass, the driver would pass some money into the customs official's hand. Quicker than light, the money would disappear into his pockets. Afterwards, he would signal to his colleagues, who would remove the plank and wave the driver on.

.... Finally, they got to Lagos mainland and the passengers began to disembark. The woman with the small bag of rice tapped the driver on the shoulder, saying to him:

"I beg, stop me for Mile Two under bridge...."

The driver screeched to a halt at Mile Two under bridge and the woman slowly rose to her feet, her large hips brushing other passengers faces as she got down from the bus. They all watched her with eyes full of compassion, her voice still ringing in their ears:

"Na small rice for my pickin."

The woman moved a little distance away from the bus and began to loosen the wrappers around her waist as if she needed to tie them more securely. She calmly let her top wrapper fall to the ground. She quickly loosened her second wrapper. And her large hips became a big bag of polished Thailand rice falling to the ground......

Woman of the Market Place

The two women climbed down from the jeep and began to walk resolutely to the banks of the murky lagoon. They leaned toward each other conspiratorially. The wind roamed in the space between their legs, swirling the sand into their shoes. The breeze dived under their boubous, whipping them into large balloons. The lagoon stretched long and wide, a weak algae colour. Little islands stuck out their thumbs. The water gurgled lazily, lapping at the green grass and the bull frogs flirting in the dusk.

The wooden houses on slits invited the two women, the rancorous laughter of half drunk men filtered out, daring the two women, "come on in, come on in, have some fresh fish pepper soup and hot ogogoro". The women hastened their footsteps, away from the huts, towards the market, that court of women where smoked fish ruled on rows and rows of wooden trays. Women bantered their evening stories, children with running noses teased each other. Toddlers played at the water's edge. No mother fretted. If the children did not fall into the lagoon, how would they learn to swim?

A trader hailed the two women, her long hair styled like a Lagos bridge swayed upon her head, precariously.

"My customers, it's been a long time. Where have you been?"

"We've been in town. How are your children?"

"They are fine. We are only battling hunger. Business has been slow."

"Do you have 'Osan fish'?"

"No, Osan is scarce these days but I've got Catfish and King of the River? Isn't it a wedding you want it for? King of the River is a good substitute."

She raised a large dried fish and turned it to face the evening sun. Sun rays glinted off the coiled, shining fish. The fish eyes sparkled, an almost reawakening. The two women each reached out a hand to take the fish. The weight surprised them. The fish nearly crashed onto the ground. One of them quickly steadied it with her right hand.

"See, I told you. It's very big," laughed the market woman.

"How much is it?"

"One thousand, five hundred naira."

"Ha, it is too expensive."

The older woman pulled her friend aside and whispered into her ear.

"What do you think? The fish is quite big."

"But we shouldn't buy it for more than six hundred."

"I think so too."

They walked back to the trader.

"We like your fish but it is too expensive. Let's take it for six hundred."

The trader turned on them angrily.

"Please, leave my fish and carry yourselves somewhere else. Do you think l stole the fish? How can you price a big fish, a whole 'King of the River' for a paltry six hundred naira. You don't have to eat the 'King' you know. Go look for bony 'shawa' fish...leave my fish!"

She let out a shrilling hiss. The women hurried away from her stall, ignoring the neighbouring traders who tugged at their clothes. The aroma of smoked fish hung in the air. A marine colony, betrayed and smoked to feed human whims and soup pots. Snake fish, Frog fish, Catfish, water snails, periwinkles, crabs, Tilapia, Kings and Queens of the river lay spread out on various tables.

"Auntie!"

"Madam!"

"Customer!"

"I have sweet fish, freshly roasted fish. Come and see. A taste will convince you."

The women walked to the end of the row and stopped in front of a pregnant trader.

"Do you have Osan fish?"

"Yes. I have a few left. It's very hard to find now."

She pulled two dark brown fish from the bottom of her pile, two times the size of a sumo wrestler's hand.

"Here is the Osan fish, feast for bride and groom. If you are buying for a wedding, may the bride and groom have a happy marriage. May their life together be as delicious as the Orange Fish. May this new couple find favour, like the Osan fish, in the sight of every one."

"Amen. Thank you. How much is it?"

"It's only nine hundred naira."

"We did not come to the market to play price games. We really want to buy your fish but it is too expensive. Let us have it for six hundred naira.

"My friends, I know you want it for a wedding and I am a newly married woman myself. I want the young couple to enjoy the Osan fish but it is rare these days. Ask anyone. They'll tell you. Osan fish has become gold. This is the last of my stock. You can have it for seven hundred."

"We all know that money is hard to come by. We are all eating naira now but please, reduce the price for us. Let us pay six hundred. Let us meet each other half way."

The trader lifted the fish, pulled down the corners of her mouth and shrugged her shoulders.

"I'm just selling it to you because you need it for a wedding. Bring the money…"

The fish seller was tying the money in a knot in her wrapper when a cry rang out.

"Watch out! She is coming!"

The cry spread out like motorcycle outriders heralding the passage of men who trampled on human beings. Whips suddenly appeared all over the market place, in the hands of traders. The lean branches of trees, stripped of all leaves. The personage announced by the cry lurched on unsteady feet, her long hair cloaked with sand and bits of debris. Her thin legs, cracked white with dryness, held up her large, naked protruding tummy. An ostrich woman. Her breasts, shaped like large green mangoes half sagged on her chests. Only a pink undergarment attempted to safeguard her vagina. She moved like a song of chaos, unorchestrated. The violins going crazy. The guitar strings about to snap. The conductor at the end of his mind.

She swayed from stall to stall, her rogue gaze intent on the fish. She held out her hands in a gesture of begging. No trader left her empty. Some gave her gifts of fish, others poured abuse on her, threatening her with whips, away from their fish tables. The three women at the end of the row watched her come. One of the women turned and asked the trader,

"But who could have made this poor woman pregnant?"

"A market night watch man."

"A night watchman? Hired to guard the property of women?"

"Yes. He raped her."

"He dared to rape a madwoman of the market place?"

"Have you forgotten the proverb, 'the one we begged to scratch our backs has thorns in his hands.....?'"

"How was he found out?"

"He was found on top of her in the early hours of morning by farmers bringing fresh vegetables to the market."

The deranged woman rambled to the end of the row, muttering,

"I just came from England yesterday. I met the queen. She was very kind to me. Thank you, those who gave me fish to eat. I have a car. It's at the mechanic's. The silly mechanic. He said the car will be here by morning. I think I'll just use my aeroplane instead. I will fly down and give him a surprise. Give me fish, give me food. Don't let a woman starve. I killed him. I told him not to do it anymore. I did not like him. Woman, sister, give me fish".

The trader gave her a piece of fish and some money. She

clutched her booty to her chest and turned in the direction from which she had come.

'Why did you give her money?," one of the woman asked.

"It is business as usual in the market place. They will sell her food if she has money."

"You said the farmers found them together in the morning. Was the night guard so sex crazed, he slept the whole night with her?"

"You heard her with your own ears. She killed him. He was naked and stone-cold the following morning....A heavy stone stained with blood nestled between their inter-twined legs."

"May be some one else killed him...."

"No, they found her spread eagled, her arms flung out, the way one sleeps after accomplishing a difficult mission. They removed the man. His semen had dried on her thighs. The women covered her up and called the police. The police took away the dead man and administered a sedative to the sleeping woman. The police took her away."

"Was she ever brought to trial?"

"No, you know how the Nigerian police is..."

"Did the police release her without giving her psychiatric care?"

"They couldn't have released her. She must have escaped. She showed up yesterday. Her time is near. I think she couldn't resist the lure of the market place."

The three women watched the pregnant woman as she stumbled and staggered, her feet finding the stones of the market place like a baby groping for her mother's breast. She knew every smell in her path. Her stomach was heaving. Suddenly, she cried out, "I killed him!" Her birth waters broke. She fell on her knees. The seed of a rapist and a madwoman was bearing fruit. This was her birth position as the shouting, excited, frantic market women gathered round her.

Someone is Beating a Woman

The traffic jam snaked on for nearly a kilometer on both sides of the road as if a major catastrophe had happened. I began to play a game of guess work, wondering what could possibly be wrong. It certainly could not be fuel shortage.

Like bees from the bee hive, people were pouring out of Molue buses and out of their cars. Only the Okada riders kept weaving their motorcycles dangerously through spaces so paper thin, a mosquito could barely fly through, ignoring the rivers of abuse flowing after them.

The other passengers in the bus I was in were beginning to climb down with an annoying eagerness. All headed to watch whatever spectacle might be responsible for this traffic jam. Some of them were running as if there were free gifts ahead they must not miss. From my vantage front seat, they looked like a festive crowd in their multicoloured clothing.

I could not risk getting down to join the crowd. I was carrying five thousand naira in my bag, money I had nearly starved to save for my house rent. And it was common knowledge that a spectacle watching crowd drew expert Lagos pick-pockets like sugar drew ants. I hugged my bag tight and poked my head out of the window to ask a middle aged woman returning from the scene what the traffic delay was all about.

"Some men were beating a woman", she replied. My heart began to pound in my ribs.

"But why! What did she do?"

"They said she was a thief. The woman was shouting, insisting that she was not a thief. She said she was only trying to clear the traffic because her sick brother in a car stuck behind several cars in the traffic jam needed to be rushed to hospital." Her other brothers heard her screaming, they ran out of the car and ferociously turned on her attackers. Now it has become a free for all fight. The police has only just arrived."

Another man passed by muttering, "Lagos, it's so full of the absurd…."

It sounded crazy. Why would anyone beat a woman simply because she was trying to clear the traffic so her sick brother could be taken to hospital?

What had caused the original traffic jam she wanted to clear? The woman answering my questions had already moved on. I decided to go and investigate for myself………

Deftly, I removed my money from my bag and tucked it inside one of my bra cups for safekeeping. Whoever intended to steal the money would need to grab my breast. My aunt, a pharmacist had once told me that this method was dangerous to women's health, because the mercury on the money could cause breast cancer. I reasoned that ten minutes wouldn't do any harm. I briskly opened the door of the bus and hit the side walk. I ran towards the crowd and stood shock still at the sight that met my eyes.

The woman's braids were the colour of sand mixed with engine oil. Her eyes were swollen. She was wiping blood from her face and was nearly totally naked. Her orange T- shirt had been torn with intense force. Her bra straps were also torn. Miraculously, the cups were still in place over her breasts. Her jeans Capri shorts had also been ripped. She was seated on the side walk, weeping profusely and telling her story to the crowd gathered around her. She could not have been more than twenty five years old.

People were gathered around her, shaking their heads and trying to console her. The policemen were having a herculean time trying to stop her brothers who seem determined to beat her attackers to death. One of the women around removed her head scarf and wrapped it round the girl's chest to shield her from the ogling eyes of the men gathered in the crowd. Another draped a second scarf over her shoulders.

"… I told them my brother was very sick. I had never seen them before. I was only trying to clear the traffic jam.

A motor cyclist had hit a Mercedes Benz car and the two men were shouting at each other in the middle of the road instead of moving aside to let the traffic flow. I went up to them and asked them to move their vehicles, so that the traffic can flow freely. I told them that my brother was very sick and we were rushing him to hospital. Is that a crime, asking them to allow other people to use the road?"

"The big man in the white agbada was the one who first slapped me. He said I should shut up. Who did I think I was, a small girl to talk to him like that…. How dare I ask him to remove his car… His fat wife also rushed out of their Mercedes and began to abuse me. She called me a whore…"

Again, she burst into sobs, some people in the crowd began to calm her, coaxing her gently, so they could hear the end of her story:

"These big men like to take laws into their own hands as if Nigeria was their father's property. They think they can mistreat the poor, anyway they choose."

"Don't cry. Your brothers have given them a good beating, they will ache for days."

"The silly men, they were beating you just because you are a woman. They should have taken on a man their size. They must have their head examined."

The policemen had finally managed to restrain her brothers. The big man's wife was cowering in the shade of a tree, kept in protective custody by a policeman at her side. Her garish golden sunglasses lay smashed on the tarmac.

"And the big man and his wife began to call me a thief. They said I was clearing the road for my gang. They removed my earrings, my wristwatch, my necklace. They tore my T shirt, pounding my body with their fists. See blood all over me. They wanted to bundle me inside the Mercedes car. I kept screaming for my brothers…"

She began to tremble in a fresh flood of tears as the traffic jam started thawing in a trickle.

The Job Trail

They were sitting around the charcoal stove, huddling round the fire for warmth. Drenched in green gutter slime, my wet clothes clinging to my body, I call to them for help. Could they kindly give me a bowl of water to wash the grime crawling all over my skin? Their silence is a thick wall. They gaze at my distress with nonchalant eyes and go on drinking their tea and talking in their high pitched voices.

I walk away from them, searching in my bag for handkerchiefs, tissue paper, writing paper, anything at all that could be used as a cleaning agent. I check my wristwatch. It has stopped working. How was I going to be on time for the interview? I began to clean my body and my clothes as best as I could with some scrunched up tissue paper I retrieved from my bag while trying as much as I could to protect myself from the rain with my battered umbrella.

The rain this morning had been very heavy and it was still drizzling in irritating drops. Impeded by choked gutters and inadequate drainage, some streets in Apapa had rapidly flooded with rain water. One moment, I was walking comfortably in a few centimeters of rain; by the next, I had plunged straight into a gutter.

How could I show up at the interview looking like a slice of bread soaked in green slime? I thought about the habitual contents of Apapa gutters: urine, spit, fruit peels, engine oil, human feaces, dead rats and just about whatever it could take, parts of which were now on my body. I felt my stomach retch but I forced the nausea down. I could not afford to throw up my breakfast. I had no money for lunch.

I had been trekking the streets for six months with a biology degree, for a job nobody wanted to give, despite my wisely investing in a friendship with the newspaper vendor down my street. Akpan, the vendor liked me and allowed me the privilege of reading the papers for as long as I could bear to stay under the sun, in front of his little table. I became an esteemed member of his 'Free Readers' Association' which was how I learnt about this job opening for a receptionist. The only qualifications required were a School Leaving Certificate, ability to speak good English and good interpersonal skills.

The employment agency I had tried wanted some money before they would accept me as a client.... Where would I find the money? I decide to apply for the lower status job than starve with my university degree. I had sailed through the first interview panel. Today's was the second and the interviewer was the chairman of the company. I borrowed some little bits and pieces from my sisters and friends to make a good impression and now all my borrowed clothes, shoes, bag, perfume were all drenched. I ask a passer by what time it was and I discover I have just one hour to make it to the interview.

I walk slowly, confused, angry and very close to tears. I see a woman walk to the front of her shabby house with boxes of soap, matches and a tall wooden stool. She puts down the stool and balances a tray on it. She begins to arrange her bars of caustic soda soap, match boxes and different coloured sweets.....I walk up to her:

"Good morning, Madam. I beg, I get small problem... I get interview now, now. As I dey waka go de place, I fall for inside gutter..., I beg you fit help me get iron, make I dry my cloth?"

She looks me up and down suspiciously, trying to authenticate my story. My sorry state convinces her and she kindly invites me into her home. She plugs an electric iron for me and gives me a wrapper to wrap round my body while the iron dries my clothes. I thank her with all my heart. I switch the iron to maximum heat, nearly scorching my clothes. I iron very rapidly, drying shirt and skirt as much as I could, hearing the clock in the woman's home tick tocking the minutes away. I dress quickly and hurry out, stopping to thank the woman:

"Madam, thank you o, na you save me today, thank you."

"My sister, we thank God. Go well!"

Sent on my way with her good wishes, I walk at a near run and arrive at the imposing offices of Frank and Co. Nigeria Limited in the nick of time. An office assistant ushers me into the secretary's office. She smiles at me.

"You are right on time"

I return a weak smile, saying to myself "you don't know what kind of morning I have just had."

We hear a bell ring and the secretary says, "You can go in now."

Trying very hard to relax and not to shiver from the cold of the split air conditioning units, I open the door.

The chairman looms large from behind his crafted pine wood desk. I greet him but he does not answer. He waves me into a chair and fiddles with my application forms. Authoritatively, he says, "would you wear a bikini on the beach?"

The question completely stuns me. What has being a receptionist got to do with going to the beach in a bikini? I am thrown off balance and begin to stammer:

"I'll, no, no, I am not sure I would..."

"Why didn't you use all the space you were provided with in your forms?. You wrote so little... Are you painstaking?, What makes you think you can work without supervision?

His questions are like Kungfu punches and I begin to shrivel in my seat, losing my confidence. I felt like tooth paste being crushed out of the tube...

Finally, he says, "You can go now, we may get in touch with you," I find my feet and lurch out of his office like a drunk man... down the stairs of Frank and Co. down the street, down to the bus stop, I walk in a desperate daze.

The bus stop is rowdy. The sun is really hot now and everybody seemed to be out..., some children were racing after the buses, hawking boxes of Gala sausage pies already past their sell by date. Others were poking small packets of water in every face. The noon rang with the melody of traders advertising their various wares.

"It is cold, it is so cold, it stings your teeth. Drink cold tea and kill your thirst."

"Buy bread, bread and butter, buy bread."

"Sew your shoes. The shoemaker is here."

"Hot roasted corn, hot roasted corn, come and buy."

And the bus conductors shouted their different routes.

"Aguda, Surulere, Aguda, Surulere!"

"Ikeja, Maryland, Ikeja, Maryland!"

The aroma of frying sweet potatoes and plantain assail my nostrils but I know I have only a lunch of garri and sugar awaiting me at home.

Wearily shielding my eyes from the glare of the sun, I see a gleaming Toyota Corolla car glide to a stop in front of me. I look at the car irritatingly, wondering why the driver is suddenly blocking my access to the buses. The driver smiles at me. He presses a button and the right car window glides down. His smile widens:

"Where are you going", he says. "I would like to give you a ride."

He is looking at me solicitously, as if he truly wants to give me a ride. He looks like a close up shot of the father image you would find in a Kodak commercial targeting families. The kind of man who remembers his wife's birthday, buys her card himself and is always there for his children's important events. He looks fifty-ish.

I reply, "I am going to Aguda."

"That's right on my way, come in."

Pushing to the back of my mind incidents of women killed or raped by strange men, I move towards the car, ignoring the baleful glares of the crowd under the sun, who watched and smirked as he opened the car door for me. I step into the cool interior and fasten my seat belt.

Glancing at me from the corners of his eyes, he says,

"A beautiful young woman like you should not be waiting under the sun. You should have a car of your own."

"Well, it is obvious that I do not."

"Don't you have a boyfriend? Your boyfriend should give one."

Trying to steer the conversation out of the dangerous waters it was headed, I ask him, "What do you do when you are not offering rides to women in distress, what else do you do for a living?"

"I am a civil engineer. I once worked for Delta Oil but when they passed me over for a promotion I felt I deserved and which they had led me to expect, I resigned and set up my own shop. Now I provide support for the oil industry… security and maintenance checks on their buildings and installations. Now that you know what I do, would like to have lunch with me?"

He put his hands proprietarily on my lap. I impatiently flick them away.

"No, thank you. I have an appointment to catch soon."

My stomach growled with hunger but I knew from the language of his hands and his voice that he would give me a bill for the 'free' lunch. And it would be a price I had no wish to pay. I did not wish to be a side-kick for an oil executive's lunch time. My face hardens. Again, he puts his hand on my lap and lightly caresses.

I firmly grip his hand and place it with a resounding slap on his thigh, saying to him, "Please keep your mind on the road and your hands on the wheel."

He looks at me sternly,

"If you knew you weren't going to play the game, why did you enter my car? I did not force you. It was your choice."

I kept mute, knowing that I had indeed made a foolish choice. An oppressive silence descended in the car. We both kept our eyes on the road. He pulled to a halt at a bus stop midway to Aguda and barked at me. "Get out".

I fumbled with the seat belt, loosening it with shaking hands. I open the door quickly and climb out. He leans over to pull the car door shut. With a last disdainful glance at me, he sped off, showering me with stagnated water and images of kind Kodak fathers going to rot.

Flickering Flames

How was I born on the red laterite soil, on the corn husk littered ground? How did I sniff the earth? The tangy, acrid smell of it? These are questions l like to ask myself in my quest for answers. The varying versions, the different ruminations for truth all help to stretch and exercise my mind. The path one treks into the market is not crucial. What counts is the arrival itself. You can ask my mother. On Friday morning, she takes the south path in to the market because of the 'Ajo'. My mother is the market 'Ajo' money collector, the bank of ten market women.

Every Friday armed with her little blue exercise book and red biro, she would start with Mama Risi who sold hot fried 'puff puff' doughnuts to the school children, working her way through the circuits and turns of the market place from woman to woman, stall to stall collecting the weekly one hundred naira, the women in her cooperative had saved up. Skipping a puddle here, nearly slipping on a banana peel there.

At the end of the month, she would give the accursed nest egg of ten women to whoever was in line to take the money for the month. My mother's service charge was five percent of the total sum, payable each month by the recipient. In this way, the market women were able to raise capital to increase their stock of goods, pay their children's school fees and meet whatever other need arose in their families.

On other days she entered the market by the east route, close to Baba Soji's shop who sold nails, metal locks and cans of cheap paint that peeled off walls after three heavy rains and five bouts of hot sunshine. But if she hit her left foot on a stone at the entrance to the market, she would enter by the north path to ward off all bad luck, muttering under her breath, "I am not food for the road, I am not walking on a day when the road is hungry. I reject every bad luck. Good luck, good luck, come my way today. Come forth."

So you see, my mother always ended up at her stall in the market, a little wooden shed, conjured up from left over timber planks and rusty nails, its tin roof leaking in several spots. I loved it when it rained. I always longed to crawl out and wallow in the mud. But mother was always quick to pick me up, deftly carrying me on her back, wrapped in her sweat and spices scented wrapper. I long for the day when I would be old enough to outrun her and escape into the rain.

…Three days before I was born, my father made love to my mother. I think this must have had something to do with the suddeness of my birth. I had overheard Mama Toke, my mother's aunt warning her to keep off sex two months before my expected date of delivery…But the love-making was not my father's fault. My mother tempted him with her new 'Suku' hair style and her large, beguiling eyes. He even tried to resist. I remember him saying to her, "But you told me that Mama Toke said we shouldn't …..it might cause the baby to be born too early…"

My mother laughed and said "It's just one of those old wives tales… Come, my husband…" And admittedly, he was very gentle. I was not rocked at all. I felt no tumult in my warm womb nest. Maybe that adds nothing to the event of my birth but I have always wondered.

According to my mother's version, it was the fuel crisis that made her give birth like a nanny goat in the full glare of a city. The panic brought on by the flickering flames. It had in fact been a terrible day. Lagos was choking in the noose of a fresh fuel crisis. The queues at the petrol filling stations stretched for miles. The drivers sat in their hot vehicles, tired, hungry and angry. The air smelled of violence held on a leash, like a puff adder lying in wait, intending to strike. Now and again, the tension flared into fights. Men who had slept at the fuel stations, starved of sleep and their wives, relieved their frustrations on each other, viciously pummeling each other's flesh like carpet beaters whipping the dust out of carpets.

Street hawkers camped nearby, making brisk business

from selling sand tasting 'pure water', over-sugared biscuits, roasted peanuts, white bread and bottles of not so cold Coca Cola, Fanta, Limca and Krest Bitter Lemon. The soldiers swaggered around in their knobby boots, holding guns casually and dangerously. Their nonchalant aggression made everyone nervous of accidental gun discharge. They were like alcoholics strung out on heroin. Anything could happen. Sometimes, they flogged the weary drivers with horsewhips and the butt of their guns. Yet, they flagrantly bought all the petrol they wanted in large, black fifty litre jerry cans while men who had queued for days languished in the sun.

I was born on a day like this. Mother left the house at seven in the morning for her ante natal appointment scheduled for nine a.m. She sat at the bus stop for one hour, an eight months pregnant woman. No empty bus came. All the buses passing the stop were bursting at the seams. Human beings were crammed like a jar of olives, sitting or standing on every space. Finally, a bus that was half empty came, calling out "Ojuelegba! Ojuelegba! Enter with your fifty naira!", a two hundred percent increase on the normal fare. All in one week. Mother begged the bus conductor to accept a fare of thirty naira. He refused. A young man in the bus asked her to come in, saying he would pay the balance. My mother got in. The bus moved on.

After traveling some miles, it hiccupped to a stop. It had run out of petrol. A storm of abuse rose from the passengers, falling on the driver and his conductor. The conductor clambered down and removed a twenty litre can of petrol from the boot of the bus but he could not find a funnel to help him fill the fuel tank.

The passengers clamoured round him, "give me my change! You, 'coconut head'!". "Good for nothing driver, cheat! increasing transport fares for no just cause!" "Thieves, robbers, foolish men, give us our money right away or else, we'll trash you." The conductor ignored them, concentrating on a plastic bottle he picked off the road, cutting the top half into a funnel…

Mother, thankful that they had not been roasted alive and seeing that her clinic was nearby, walked the rest of the way…

As Dr Kola examined her, he remarked, "all this stress will probably bring your baby some days early…" He got one of his patients going mother's way to drive her to the market. That day, at dusk, mother closed her stall and came home to cook dinner. Entering our out house kitchen, she poured what she thought was kerosene into the stove. She re-arranged the stove rings and turned up the wick.

Then she struck a match and dropped the flaming stick into the stove rings, as she turned towards the kitchen sink. The stove exploded, shooting up a ball of fire almost into my mother's face. Only a miracle protected her and the fact that I was destined to be born.

Mother ran out into the courtyard, screaming, "heeellp! heeellp! fire! fire! fire!" The neighbours desperately carried buckets of water and baskets of sand. To douse the ferocious flames. Nobody near by had a telephone and the public phone booths around were all lifeless. The fire service could not be reached.

As the flames ate up our kitchen, my mother's birth waters broke. I was impatient. I no longer wanted the primordial lake of the womb. I wanted a role in the drama. Why shouldn't I join the neighbours, battling the flames in my mother's kitchen. I moved my head into her pelvis. I tucked my chin under. I pressed my strong willed shoulders on her body tissues and faxed my mother's brain a staccato message, 'push! open up!'

The contractions began. Mother collapsed into a neighbour's arms, hanging tight and screaming my father's name. Behind us, the fire reigned. I would not be held back. I must salvage the kitchen. Riding on the waves of mighty contractions, I push through my mother's vagina, tearing it. I fell polp with bloody gook and yuck into neighbours arms on the sun baked earth, surrounded by a gawking crowd of never–mind–their–own–business Lagosians. I opened my mouth and yelled at the flickering flames licking its lips on the ashes of my mother's kitchen.

The Weeping Child Laughs Again

The sound of hammer on the nails gives Rita a good feeling. She is making impact. She is getting a response. The hammer fits snugly into her hand. She wields it anyway she chooses. It is her show and hers is all the action. She leans back and surveys the shinning nails now transfixed in her walls. They had better hold or else she would replace them. She had a lot more nails in store.

Rita lifts the large painting and gently nestles it in the arms of nails. The nails embrace the painting. They hold up. She looks around at all the work of her hands and she thinks that it is good. The maroon brocade curtains, the multi-coloured straw mat on the terrazzo tilled floor, the dried flowers in a purple mug, her brown four-seater settee and *The Weeping Child Laughs Again*. The artist had looked puzzled when she commissioned the painting. "Make me a weeping child," she said, "let her laugh again." The artist asked, "what emotion will be the over riding impulse of the work?"

"Sadness and joy", she answered. He looked at her intently, trying to read her heart in the lines between her words but he only met an impersonal stare. Unsearchable eyes set in a calm face. Her eyes said to him, "it is my money. It is my choice." He shrugged his shoulders and said, "I will call you when it is ready."

...Now the painting was upon her brown like the freshly upturned earth walls. *The Weeping Child Laughs Again*. The painting spoke of thunder, of blood and laughter. It had a hint of beach sand. Swallows flying above a tumultuous sea. The red and purple, the contortions of yellow and blue and stark white threw up the face of a girl child gazing out to sea. Her tears are drying up on her face or perhaps they shall just begin to pour. Maybe she is calling on her water resources, summoning up the liquid within her, like a Lagos homemaker turning her kitchen taps and frantically hoping she would not have to leave her second floor apartment to ferry water in a bucket from the basement tap.

The child's eyes are set on a nearly invisible canoe on the ravaging sea. There is someone that cannot be seen in the water. The child's mother on her way home from a market trip across the ocean. The child's eyes are brimming over with hope. My mother is a good swimmer, she thinks, she has abandoned the leaking canoe. She is in the water, swimming towards me. The beginnings of laughter are on her lips…Mother is swimming like a fish. The fish cannot eat her.

Rita loves this painting. It is the crowning piece of her living room décor. The painting speaks to her. It says see how far you have traveled. See the thunder that could not kill you. You are a serious survivor…

Rita remembers walking into the school chapel, when she was eight, at five in the afternoon. And her petition on her knees, begging God to spare her mother's life.

Yetunde, her mother had married her father, Bode, soon after she finished secondary school. In those days, any girl who had a secondary school leaving certificate was considered very well educated. Her father was the desire of the village girls. He had a Hanson bicycle which he rode at top speed, his shirt flying in the wind. He had asked Yetunde to marry him because he wanted an educated woman who would also know her place and never talk back to him.

Rita's grandmother had warned, "Young lady, think very carefully. Don't squander yourself. There is no known trait of insanity in their family but they are bad tempered. His father is a wife beater."

Her mother, drunk on love, replied, "Mama, Jide told me he had a dream. He was chasing a crowd of women with a long, thin 'Pankere' cane. He ran and ran after the women, whipping any woman he met with his 'Pankere'. I was among the fleeing women. At a corner where the path bent and trailed away into the distance, he said I stopped and quit running. My other friends were shouting, 'Mosun, run! run! he is going to beat you.' I said no, he would not. And then he found himself pulled by a force he could not conquer, moving towards me like a magnet to metal. Reverently, he gave me the cane like a bouquet of flowers and l graciously received it from him, entwining my hands in his. Then we walked away together."

Her grandmother had replied, "Remember the sayings of our people, 'the whip that was used on the first wife is waiting in the rafters for the second wife'. A whip is a whip. It can never become a bouquet of flowers. How will it take root? How will it sprout? How will the flowers bud? You better take care."

In the years that came, Yetunde, her mother, often said to her, "I wish I had listened to my mother. A girl can have as many clothes as an old woman but she cannot have as many rags."

Rita's father used her mother as his regular exercise. He loved to punch her up. Rita remembers the night when as a child of six, she had screamed and woken up the whole neighborhood because she thought it was her mother's last night on earth. Her father has hit her mother on the head with the stilletto pointed tips of her high heels. Blood spurted out. Her mother fainted, and Rita began to scream. Her cries jerked up the neighbours from sleep. They ran into their home and took her mother to hospital, while Auntie Sola, their next door neighbour, took Rita into her house, and gave her half a tablet of paracetamol to swallow. Auntie Sola calmed her down, telling her that her mother was going to be okay. She put Rita to bed.

The next day, when she was taken to see her mother in hospital, she whispered to her, "Mummy, when you are well, let us leave daddy. We will go and live with grandma and grandpa."

Her mother just smiled and hugged her. When she got well, she did not leave Rita's father. She stuck to him like Uhu glue and got beating after beating, broken teeth and puffy eyes. Sometimes, Rita cried with her mother. She would ask her "how could you bear all the battering… he will kill you one day…"

Her mother rubbing the bald spot on her head where the hair never grew back would answer, "But I cannot leave you and your brothers and your sisters. He would not let you come with me. I have to stay for your sake. I cannot leave my children."

Sometimes, her mother fought back. With her words. Sometimes, her tongue cut Rita's father, piece meal by piece meal, spewing out curses, family secrets:

"Useless man, you slap me in front of my children because of a gas cooker I bought with my own money…you've kept beating me all the years I have slaved for you. You keep kicking me like a football. Since the birth of our youngest son, two years ago, you have not slept with me. May you never prosper, may you fall and never rise, may your enemies prevail against you…"

Wiping her mother's tears with the hem of her little frock, tears steaming down her own face, Rita would try to muffle the curses, she would try to stem her father's ire, covering her mother's mouth with her little girl hand.

Nowadays, Rita has an eye for women like her mother even when they wore a cloak of make up and designer perfume. They were broken into, like sardine tins, their eyes washed out with countless tear drops. They looked like just blown out candle wicks, barely smoking. They were tall thin pine trees, buffeted by a driving wind with an interior of steel that could be summoned as a desperate remedy.

When Rita was in her early twenties, her mother bought a house with a government loan, a refuge for the day her father would finally throw her suitcase out. Her mother's uncle stood surety for her and helped her process the necessary papers. They kept the news away from her father until all the mortgage papers were signed. On hearing the news, he smirked a 'congratulations' and shriveled up. His eyes were stunned. Where did she find the courage?

He decoded the message for what it was. I am not afraid any longer. I have a roof and a hearth snug enough to shield me. Her father began to brood around the house. Her mother bloomed and straightened her shoulders. Head held high, chest slightly thrown forward. The walk of freedom when it leaps out of shackles…Her father mumbled and wobbled, dissolving into old age….

The heavy Lagos rains recently dugs holes in the roof of her father's house. It leaked like a sponge. The family moved into her mother's house while her father's roof was being restored. After the renovations, Rita did not return with her family.

She chose to live in her mother's house. A cheerful little bungalow, where her paintings have room to breathe. See Rita reclining on her settee. She has a can of diet coke in her hands. She is smiling and looking at *The Weeping Child Laughs Again*. She knows her mother is swimming through the waves. She is coming home to her. The fish will not tear her flesh. She will soon knock on the front door.

Joker Card

It seems to be oil sizzling in the pan. The onions embrace the oil, the blended peppers follow. The wind is scented. Bose's daughter can be heard behind the wooden partition, stirring the sauce in the pan. See her cooking, how she adds the locust beans after the sauce has heated a little. She crumbles the seasoning cube, she adds salt, fine like talcum powder, the soup bubbles on the fire.

Watch how she pours the hot sauce on her bare palms. How she quickly licks it off. Picture her cooking. The aroma is borne like a gift to your nostrils because of the gossiping wind.

Outside the shop, a hen and her chicks are foraging for worms. The wind ruffles their tail feathers, a hawk suddenly swoops, claws ready to snatch a chick. The hen lets out a clatter, cluck, clack, cluck, cluck. The children are distracted from their play. They happily pick up stones, joyfully targeting the fleeing hawk. A baby flaps her dimpled hands. She is about to put her mud pies in her mouth; her mother snatches her up, wiping her runny nose.

Through all of these, Bose has not stirred. She seats on her swivel chair, unmoving. There is not much she can do within the confines of her grey blouse and wrapper. She is wearing no jewelry. Her face is lean, like an abandoned homestead crumbling at the pillars. A woman pulls aside the glass doors and steps into the shop.

"Good afternoon, I would like to retouch my hair?"

"Come in and sit down. Yinka," she shouts to her daughter. "Come and plug the boiling ring."

The woman settles into a large, white plastic chair. Bose walks to a small blue bucket holding various combs and picks out a large-toothed comb. She begins to comb the woman's hair, mechanically, her mind trailing off...

"If I die, be sure to keep your wits about you. Be on the alert. Keep your eyes sharp and focused. Let them rest on the television, and the furniture, and the car and the land deed. If anyone from my family wants to remove things from the house, don't let them." He had laughed then, mimicking a tearful voice.

"Stop joking with death, you are going to live and see your children's children," she had retorted. She pulled at the lady's hair. The woman's yell of pain jerked her back to the present.

"Sorry, madam, I am really sorry. Yinka, pour some water into the steaming bottle and plug the steamer."

She gently untangles all the knots out of the woman's hair and places a towel round her shoulder. The woman rises from her chair and walks across the room to a throne like chair, sturdily built on a little raised platform. The carpenter, who made the chair, in a fit of inspiration had etched 'princess' onto the back of the chair. He felt any woman who sat on it would feel extra pampered like a real princess just by sitting on his chair.

She scoops warm water from a bowl and pours it onto the woman's hair. She begins to wash. She misses him most when she washed wet hair with shampoo. It felt like his hands on her body, soft and gentle, going and moving wherever she wanted them to move. She feels like one bottled down hunger. What would a woman used to good sex two or three times a week do in her sudden widowhood?

Trying to stir up a frenzy of forgetting, she rinses the woman's hair and roughly towel-dries it. The woman stands up, walks back to her former chair and opens a little plastic bag. She brings out bottles of hair moisturizers, whose labels read like a procession of gardens, Chamomile extract, rosemary extract, comfrey, white nettle, sage, aloe vera oil. The woman hands the bottles to her. She pours a little of each on her hair, messages her scalp with circular motions, caps her with a transparent plastic cap and sends her under the steamer.

She returns to her chair, to the lure of memory, tramping in the bush with no pathways.

He had a headache that refused to yield to analgesics. He went to the office clinic. The doctor said, "It is a psychosomatic disorder brought on by intense stress. Mr. Laolu, you work too hard. I must place you on a one-week bed rest."

He had grumbled and complained but she firmly agreed with the doctor and would not even let him come home. She had packed a few clothes and toiletries and taken them to him at the hospital. She protected him from concerned family members and friends who wanted to come visiting, saying "He is fine really. He is just on a little bed rest. The doctor says he mustn't see anybody, and his doctor is quite strict. Doctors orders have got to be obeyed." She would close her shop early and spend time with him in the evening, teasing him and piling him with jokes on how rest agreed with him and may be it was time to take that vacation to Ghana.

Three days into his bed rest, he was gone. He just slept on. He would not wake when the nurses tried to rouse him. He did not wake when she clutched him at the hospital, crying his name, crying his nickname, crying his family's poetic salutations specially taught her by his grandmother. He just slept on. She did not know how she got home. She did not know she slept. She remembered no dreams. She woke up the next morning and only knew she wanted to die.

Her screaming woke up her younger sister and her best friend who were sleeping on her left and on her right. They stood up in a flash and held her. She did not know how they got there or how they had put her to bed, watching her like guardian angles. She began to cry, great sobs wrenching out her guts like a volcano bursting at the seams. Yetunde said to her, "Remember your children." That sentence hit her like a ray of intense sunlight and dried up her tears.

She turned to her sister, "where are my children?" Her sister replied, "I have taken them to our parents. They are being looking after."

A knock on the door startled the three women. Whoever was knocking turned the door handle and walked in, barely giving her time to straighten her nightdress. He strode up to her with her husband's briefcase in his hands, her husband's special leather crafted brown briefcase, the one he kept important documents in.

"Good morning, our wife, we are all in shock, everybody is distressed, our calabash is broken, our oil is eaten up by the desert"…he paused to wipe the corners of his eyes, "But we all have to be strong for the sake of the children… there is a family meeting this evening at six to discuss the funeral arrangements."

She saw her husband's words rise up before her eyes, "Keep your eyes dry, sharp and focused."

She said to her brother-in-law, "what are you doing with my husband's briefcase?"

"Ha, our wife, it is my brother's briefcase. Do not question my right to it. I am just trying to sort out his papers for your good and for the good of your children." Turning on his heels, he walked out of the room and left the door open.

Her sister rose up to shut the doors, turning to say to her, "my sister, do not fight with them, take it easy, I do not want them to hurt you or the children."

Her best friend hugged her, saying, "you have to be strong and careful. Remember the struggle my sister had when she lost her husband. If you fight them head on, they can throw you out of the house –I do not think Gbenga made a will, did he?"

"No," she had replied, he had not planned to die at forty.

"Even if he had left a will, there are no guarantees. So, you see, you have to be very careful. You have to walk in wisdom. If you decide to take them to court, there are no real laws protecting the rights of widows and the judge can be bribed. You have to be really careful. Calm down and let's plan. Thank God, you have you own business. You will not have to depend on them for food."

Her friend continued. "You know, when my sister's husband died, his older brother wanted to inherit her and make her his second wife. We were all shocked to the bone by this supposedly enlightened man. When she refused him, he lobbied the rest of his family to say, they would only look after two of her six children unless she married him."

"My sister said to them, 'what about the remaining four? Are they bastards?, aren't they your brother's children?' No-one answered her. My sister, called their bluff, rose up and walked out of the meeting with all her children. You know how difficult it has been for her, working day and night at her grocery shop, stretching ends, often going without food, so her children could eat. It's been very hard. But now, four of her children are out of university. Be prepared to work extra hard, the signals I can sense from your in-laws don't look good."

Dry-eyed and calm, she had attended the evening meeting, still flanked by her sister and her best friend. After praying for the repose of the soul of their dead brother, her husband's older brother had opened up the proceedings, merely informing her of the decisions they had taken about her life and her children's:

"Our wife, it is indeed a very tragic time for us all. Our wonderful brother left us without saying farewell. Our pillar is broken. Our house has come crashing down. The elephant is fallen but we must look after his legacy. We must look after you and the children he left behind, his five children."

At the number five, she jerked up her head in surprise, she and Gbenga had four children. Could the old man's grief have quickly dimmed his memory? His voice went on:

"Our wife, 1 can see that you didn't know your husband had another child by another woman. A daughter, she is three years old."

"Are you sure of what you are saying? Where is the child?"

"Our wife, Gbenga told us about the child as soon as she was born. Some of us even followed him to the naming ceremony at Ibadan. He didn't want to tell you. He said he did not want to hurt you. Here is a photo of the child."

He handed it to her. She saw her husband's trumpet shaped nose on the child's face. She saw his eyes mocking her behind the child's smile. She slowly handed the photo back to the old man, too stunned to be angry.

She could see the future before her eyes, she saw jagged mountains, the shark infested waters, the mosquitoes humming for blood, the knives seeking her flesh and in the well of her grief, she had reached deeply for grace to be strong.

The old man droned on. "We have checked his papers; he made Ayo, your first-born child, his next kin. He is the one authorized to collect his father's life insurance cheque from the company. The insurance company has given us an appointment for next week Tuesday. Send word to your parents and make sure that the boy is ready to go with us to collect the cheque."

"Then we shall cash the cheque and decide on the best financial plan for the children's education and your support."

Minutes before their meeting with the insurance company, she had held her shivering, fifteen-year-old son and whispered in his ears. "Bring the cheque to me."

Two of Gbenga's brothers had accompanied her and her son to the insurance company. They all sat on one side of the long table in the conference-room. The men hemmed in the boy on both sides, as if he was a treasured criminal just arrested by policemen.

The Insurance company manager expressed his condolences and extended the cheque to her son. As the boy's hands took the cheque, his uncles' hands shot up on both sides to take the cheque from him. The boy deftly elbowed his uncles and swiftly handed the cheque to his mother. Furious and smiling, she lovingly nestled the cheque in her brassiere.

Little Men

I do not know why my brother treats me like a little kid. I am ten years old and that is quite grown up. After all, my mother sends me to the market to buy things and I just got a double promotion in school. My mother was very happy. She said I had saved her one year's school fees. I studied very hard, I even read with candlelight when the electricity was cut.

At first, when the headmistress announced the promotions, I did not hear my name and I was very worried and then I heard my name. My class mates were very jealous. They started saying I must have stolen someone else's brain to pass the exams. How can I steal someone's brain....l am only ten years old.

I was very unhappy with the things they said but I did not tell my brother. He would have reported to the principal and the principal would have punished them. When I told my mother, I got a double promotion. She brought me different things including a toy film projector. She started giving me money every day to buy biscuits. My brother never got a double promotion, although he is very brilliant.

I have a bank account. I have two thousand naira in it. It is a secret. Let me run in and bring you the savings book and card.....See, I have two thousand naira in it. My uncle gave it to me. He is rich. He gave my mother twenty thousand naira and my brother and sister five thousand naira each. I got two thousand naira because l am the youngest. My money is in the bank. I cannot touch until l am eighteen. I will not touch it until I am thirty-two and then, l will give the money to my mother.

When I grow up, I want to help little children. I see so many children on the streets. There is this little boy who sits by the road side. I see him every morning on my way to school. He is always looking hungry. I think he is about seven years old. He is not as dark as I am and he has curly hair, like the Fulani people. He is always wearing dirty shorts and a torn T shirt. I see him shivering in the mornings when it is cold. His hands shakes when he holds out his beggar's bowl. The boy has very sad eyes.

Sometimes, if l am not hungry, I put my lunch money into his bowl. I also see some mothers and their twin children under the sun, begging for money. Auntie, why do these women put their children under the hot sun? Is it true that a traditional native doctor divined that the twins want their mothers to beg? But they are babies, how can they say what they want?. One day, l saw a man put five naira into their beggar's bowl. The wind blew the money into the gutter, their mother left the children and went to take the money from the gutter. A speeding taxi splashed rain water on the babies and they started crying. Their mother, too, burst into tears.

Would you like some oranges? My mother bought some and I washed them all and put them in the fridge. Do not worry, you can have them all. Are they cool enough? My uncle also gave us this fridge. You see, my father married another wife because he wanted more children. He directs cars on the road. What do you call people who points traffic in the direction they should go? Traffic wardens...? Yes, that is what he is ...

There is a boy in my class. He is our class bully. He makes us afraid. He asks us to bring him money and food. We cannot eat our lunch freely. He is always seizing our food... One day, he asked me, "Jide, wetin spoil Lagos?"

I replied, "Bribe."

"Good," he said. "You must bring me a 'bribe' tomorrow."

He wanted me to buy him off or else I would get a beating from him. The next day, I acted very ill, telling my mother that I was too sick to go to school...

God has saved my life several times. I will never forget when I was nine years old and I was almost hit by a car. My cousin caused it. He thought I could come home from school by myself but I could not. On my way home, I tried to cross the road. I ran across the road. Suddenly, a car screeched to a halt and l fell down. People gathered round and started shouting. I fell unconscious....

… I just heard a thud and a scream, a sound made by a voice that sounded like my friend, the school boy. The one who sometimes gave me his lunch money. I lifted my gaze from my bowl onto the road. The boy lay sprawled on the road. He lay still. I leapt onto my feet, taking care to pick my bowl, for thieves were no respecter of beggars, and l ran to the scene. A crowd had quickly gathered. Crowds. The one thing that Lagos had in abundance – crowds of people, mountains of rubble, fogs of smoke, clouds of dust, stench of smells. Lagos was crowded with everything.

I wriggled my way through the crowd and knelt in front of the boy, careful to keep my bowl in front of me. I touched him. I wanted to call his name but I did not know it. Suddenly I felt a hand lift me off him. Two men carried him into a waiting car. The doors slammed and the car sped off with him.

I walked back to my place in the dust, with my heart inside my stomach, hoping that this child who had fed, me, another child, with his lunch money would be alright.

I squat in the dust, watching the crowd slowly disperse, talking and going back to their walking, thieving, selling, doing–nothingness or whatever else they had been doing before the accident. I gaze into the distance, remembering the day I was nearly crushed under a bus tyre. I was begging that day at Ikeja bus stop, going from one bus window to another, begging the passengers seated for some money so I could eat. I stayed several minutes by one window, begging the man sitting by the window. He ignored me. I tried to touch him to get his attention but he frowned at me, saying, "if you dare touch me with your dirty hand. I will beat you so thoroughly you won't be able to tell night apart from day."

I quickly moved off and went to the next window. I smiled, when I saw a woman who usually gave me money sitting by the window. She always reminded me of my mother who had died when I was five years old.

I smiled at her, asking her for money, she said "little boy, I will not give you money today. Why don't you go and get a job?

Go and wash plates at some bukas, they will at least give you something to eat."

I said nothing in reply. How could I explain that the money I made from begging fed my four brothers and sisters. I could find food for myself at the food bukas but they would not give me food for my family. My father drank and gambled away the stipend he earned working as a road sweeper for the local government council.

"Madam, please give me money!" I kept urging her. A man sitting beside her gave me five naira as the bus began to move out of the garage. I kept begging her but she ignored my pleas. The bus entered the traffic. I ran beside the bus, my hand holding onto the bus, gripping it by the window. I held on, hoping that she would respond to me with a gesture of affection, this woman who looked like my mother. Someone hit my hand with a newspaper, wanting me to let go. I could not. I would not.

I, who have longed for a mother for so long. The woman who usually smiled at me. The woman who often gave me money. How could she reject me today? The bus began to gather speed. I held on for dear life for a woman who could have been my mother. People began to talk excitedly in the bus:

"The boy is possessed and greedy. He has already been given money by someone in this bus."

"Woman, do you know him, are you owing him any money?"

"No," I heard her reply, "I do not know him."

She denied me. I wanted to shout, "You know me, you have often given me money." But I had to hold tight to the bus.

Other passengers began to shout.

"Driver, driver, stop the bus. Tell the bus conductor to beat him off."

"If he falls and dies, the police will arrest you."

Passers-by began to gawk at me. I only wanted a mother. The bus stopped. The bus conductor came down. He grabbed me and shook me. "What do you want?"

I opened my mouth to speak, no sounds came forth. How could I explain the loss of a mother. The burden that my father is. The mouths I have to feed in my family's leaking one room shanty. I began to cry, and plead:

"Please, ma, please, ma, please, ma!"

"Please ma for what? What do you want from the lady?"

"I want to be her son."

I saw the lady slam the window by her side. The driver began to honk impatiently.

The bus conductor said. "But she cannot take you home. She has her own children"

He hurried and jumped into the bus. The bus sped off, leaving me gazing at it with limpid, orphan eyes.

I can only hope that my friend will be alright. I hope he has a mother to look after him…

…When I woke up, I found myself in hospital. I saw a smiling nurse. She said they had found my home address written in my exercise book. She gave me some food to eat and said she would take me home. I ate the food and asked how I got to the hospital. I could only remember falling on the road. The nurse said I have been very lucky. I was almost hit by a car but the driver stepped on his brakes in the nick of time. She said I must take better care when crossing the road next time. I must look left and right and left again to be sure that the road was clear before crossing.

When we got to my home, my mother had not yet returned from work. We met my cousin who said, "Jide, why are you coming home so late?"

The nurse was very angry with him. "Be quiet!" she shouted. "Don't you know he is too young to come all that way by himself? He was nearly hit by a car, he could have died…"

I was very lucky. Really, I came close to death. Auntie, you are leaving? So soon?, I wish you could stay a little longer. Do not forget the music tapes you wanted. You can have this one also..., it is very good. It's okay... You can take it. I will tell my brother I lent you. Yes, I will not open the door for anyone else. I will speak to them through the window and ask them to leave a message...Let me see you off. Just a minute. Just a minute, let me quickly change my shirt. Remember, do not tell your mother I got a double promotion. I want to tell her myself.

Something for the Boys

"Abuja! Port Harcourt, Enugu, Kano!"

"Madam, where are you going?, Enugu?"

"Oh, back off, she's going to Abuja…"

The clamouring voices of airport touts assail me as the 'Okada' motorcycle rides to a halt outside the gate of the second terminal at the local airport.

I ask the motorcyclist, "won't you take me inside?"

"Madam, l can't go beyond this point. See the notice."

He points to a notice on the gates. In fading green paint on a white board, it read: MOTORCYCLES ARE NOT ALLOWED BEYOND THIS POINT. ALL TRESPASSERS WILL BE PROSECUTED. I clamber down and pay him. Ten hands reach to grab my luggage.

"Madam, an Abuja plane is waiting. Bring your bag."

"Don't listen to him. The Port Harcourt plane has just landed."

"I am sure you are going to Kaduna."

"Keep off my bag!" I scream at the touts.

They melt before the force of my irritation, moving away, leaving me an open path. A red sea parting into two. Swaying with my heavy bag, I stagger past the rows of parked cars towards the ticketing office of Tradesq Airlines. As I step on to the porch of the office, three men in black and white uniforms immediately accost me:

"Madam, are you going to Abuja?"

"Yes, l want to buy a ticket."

"Ha, you came too late, the plane is full."

"O, what am l going to do now? Is there any other airline going to Abuja now?"

"Madam, don't worry, we will help you. Just come with us."

"No, no, no, I don't want you to waste my time, let me find another option."

"Madam, trust us. See, we are staff of Tradesq."

Pointing at their chests, they flash their name tags at me.

"See our I.D cards. You can rely on us."

I look at the blurred photos on the unclear, laminated, name tags. I am uneasy but l decide to take the risk. How can l win if l don't venture? My assignment at Abuja was really urgent.

"Come with us, don't worry. Let's go and see the ticketing supervisor. Perhaps someone who booked earlier will not show up. You might still get a seat. Come this way."

One of the men pick my heavy bag and starts hurrying off. I hurry after him. We walk down a short corridor and veer left into a crowded room. I look round. It is the airport lounge, overflowing with travellers. Music pour from some loud speakers. Some men huddle near a television set, watching a football game. Mothers suckle their babies, friends embrace. All around me, the din of voices and mouths in motion, clamourous like a black and white Lagos bill-board.

I am slightly bewildered, wondering what we are doing at the airport departure lounge when I did not have a ticket. I run to catch up with him and grab his arm.

"Hey, what are we doing here?

"Madam, relax, I am taking you to the supervisor."

We leave the lounge, turning right again towards some wooden sheds. They look like storage cabins. About five meters to the first shed, he suddenly dumps my bag on the bare earth. He says, "Madam, wait here, let me go and call the supervisor." A minute later, he returns with two men. One of them has a lean, hungry look in his eyes. He appraises me, taking in my polished leather shoes, gold earrings and my navy blue bag with its gold tone handles.

"Madam, the ticketing supervisor is busy, he can't see you now. I am his assistant. I will attend to you and this is my assistant"…he says as he waves towards the man on his left, fawning and bowing.

"Good afternoon, madam."

"Good afternoon, I want to buy a ticket. I hear the plane is full but I was told you could help me….."

Mister 'lean look' smiles, "Yes, madam, he replies, "we can help you but you have to put some money on top of your airfare."

I give them a cocky smile, thinking to myself, "Sorry guys, you met the wrong woman. I am not going to let you fleece me and I intend to get a seat on that flight."

I look the man in the eyes.

"I am traveling on a very tight budget, I can't afford a kobo beyond my airfare."

"Haba, madam, how can you say that?"

"But it's true. Anyway, l'm not desperate to travel. I know you have another flight tomorrow morning, I will come back then."

I bend to pick my luggage. Panic creeps into their eyes.

"Madam, don't be in such a hurry to leave. Why should you go to Abuja tomorrow when you can travel in the next few minutes? The plane is landing soon and it will leave at 4:30 p.m. Try and add a little something… for the boys."

"I've told you, I don't have a kobo more."

"Madam, come here…for a minute." My solicitous bag carrier says, trying to confer with me in a corner.

"No, I am not moving from here."

He moves near me and whispers…"Madam, there is another option. Pay me four thousand naira privately and I will ensure that you get on the plane."

"No thanks, I want an official ticket."

"Madam, you can count on me, I am a staff. We are all staff."

Once again, they flash their opaque name tags.

"When it's time to board, I will arrange with the boys on the plane. You will get on the flight…"

"Didn't you hear me? I said I want an official ticket….?

"Don't be so difficult…are you traveling privately or is it an official trip?

"It's official."

"Ha, I can now understand…don't worry. Just give me the

four thousand. I would arrange a Tradesq receipt for you. You will have something to show your office accountant."

"No, thanks!" I pick my luggage and start walking away.

"Okay madam, come, come....Na wa for you o. You women. You never like to part with money."

I retort, "I work hard for my money. I don't pluck it off trees."

They led me into the wooden shed...

"Some people even come to us for help with their expense accounts. They collect their airfare allowance and decide to travel by road, keeping the bulk of the money. They come to us for official receipts to show that they traveled by air. Times are hard. Everybody is struggling to survive. We supply them used tickets with their names written in it...

Everything. If you want that, we can do it for you. It will only cost you one thousand naira."

"Listen good, I know the official ticket costs Five thousand, five hundred and thirty naira. I am not giving anybody a penny more or less."

I stand and walk towards the back door of the ticketing office...Quickly they intercept me, "Bring the money."

As I count out the money, two of them crane their neck, trying to peep into my handbag.

"Move back!" I shoo them away. Holding the money in my hands, I turn to the first man. "Here is the money. Let's go"

He stretches out his hand to collect the money but my grip on it is firm.

"Not so fast, we are buying my ticket together."

We enter the ticketing office. It is quieter than I expect.

The cashier is reading a scandal-full magazine. I hand the money to him. He places it in a currency counting machine and presses the switch. I keep an eagle eye on the numbers racing on the machine as naira notes cascade into the receptacle below. The cashier writes me a receipt. I walk over to the ticketing office.

"I want one ticket to Abuja," I shove my receipt at him, belligerently, ready for the second battle of spurious demands. He glances at my receipt and writes me an official Tradesq ticket. Politely, he hands me the ticket.

"Ma'am, have a good trip!"

I summon the grace to say thank you. I open my ticket and look at my seat number. The number is written in bold, black ink. 16C. I turn to the ticketing officer, "but your boys told me the plane was fully booked."

"There must have been a mistake. We are just three quarter full."

As I turn to leave, my furious gaze search for the 'Tradesq boys.' Not one is in sight.

Swoop

Yemi Adebunmi stared at the NewsHorn magazine in her hands, examining every minute detail of the face on the open page before her. Dominated by a hooked nose, the face had tiny tribal marks that fanned out from the corners of his mouth in an upward slant towards the cheekbones. His eye held her gaze, daring her wrath that could not kill the spirit behind his eyes.

Her gaze travelled to the lower half of the page. She laughed softly to herself, at the caption underneath the photograph – KUNLE ADEGBEMI, BARRISTER AT LAW. FRONTLINE HUMAN RIGHTS ACTIVIST. DECLARED MISSING SINCE THE 12TH OF JUNE. She lifted her legs and placed them on her desk. She leaned back in her chair, still laughing. The door handle turned for someone about to enter the room. Yemi recalled her laughter, canned it in her throat and quickly put down her legs. She smoothed her skirt, looking as prim as a secretary in a seventies British movie.

The door opened and her colleague, Bayo walked in. He looked like a would-be prize fighter who had never managed to win any belt in the wrestling ring. His large shoulders were squeezed into a jeans shirt. Yemi opened her mouth. All the canned laughter burst out, filling the air with a wind that sent the papers on her table flying.

Bayo walked to her, smiling but wearing a slightly hurt look on his face. "What is the joke about?"

She handed him the NewsHorn. He took a look at the photo in the news magazine and joined in Yemi's laughter. His laughter sounded like a car engine being kick started…

"Well, my dear, let's start the job…" Bayo said. "I hope you got the skull.

"Yes, but it was really difficult to find one. I finally got lucky at the medical store at Gbaja. It looks real enough."

"Great!"

"I also got the blood, through it is still frozen. I bought the two packets that matched his blood group".

"And his clothes?"

"I persuaded his house boy to steal some for me for the price of three thousand naira. I think we have everything we need."

"Let's get cracking…"

She got up from her chair and went to a corner of the room. She bent down and lifted a yellow plastic bucket onto a table. Except for her table which was cluttered with dusty paper files, the rest of the room looked clean and very spartan. The white walls made the room feel clinical like an operating theatre. The floor was heavily padded with a grey carpet to muffle footsteps. It had a large unshaded light bulb in the center. Four smaller light bulbs clung to each corner of the room. It was the room where persons detained by the government had their first interrogation. They would place a chair in the middle of the room directly under the large light and sit the detained person under the rude glare. It had an unsettling effect. It felt as if a stranger was reading one's intimate diary.

Yemi took a pair of scissors and cut open a bag of blood. She held her handkerchief to her nose and stepped back as the smell of human blood filled the room.

"I thought you had nerves of iron," Bayo said to her.

"Not for the smell of blood."

Bayo stepped forward and pulled on the pair of thick white gloves lying on the table. He drained some of the thawed blood into the yellow bucket. He brought out the skull and dipped it into the bowl of blood. He went to work with a large artist paint brush, carefully coating the skull with blood until there was no patch of white left. He placed the skull on a nearby aluminum tray to dry off. Then he sat down with his butcher red gloves still on, watching Yemi tear lawyer Kunle's clothes with her hands and a pair of scissors:

"Be careful. You are using too much force. You will rip the whole shirt to shreds."

"No. Don't forget I am the in-house expert on impersonation."

"Yes ma'am, but don't be over zealous with the shirt. Remember, it has to look as if lawyer Kunle got involved in a bloody fight. I can't wait to see his wife's reaction."

"I am sure she will collapse in a heap on the floor."

"That will be less than what she deserves. You know, on one of the occasions we went to pick up her husband, she had the temerity to keep John, Isaac and I waiting for several hours in the rain."

"Why didn't you seek refuge in the car?"

"We did but the rain still blew into the car. I got wet and cold and swore I would make her pay. This is my chance…"

"And those arrogant, pompous, human rights colleagues of his would certainly be floored this time."

"They would be too dazed to think."

Once again, their laughter hit the airwaves, like a loose wolf closing in for the kill. Wiping the tears of triumph from his eyes, Bayo said:

"And the best thing is, there will be nobody to take to court. They don't know we've got him. They don't know he is with us. His wife will wake up on Tuesday morning and find a skull and her husband's bloody clothes wishing her good morning."

"Poor woman…"

"Well, next time, she will learn not to keep me waiting in the rain."

"Have you briefed the police?"

"Yes, they are already on alert. As soon as his wife discovers the bloodstained skull, the journalists will descend in hordes. I have told some of the journalists in our pay to stimulate speculations and provocative news angles, suggesting that his human rights colleagues should be arrested and detained by the police for questioning and to help the police with the mystery of the skull and the blood stained clothes."

"Well done! It's a tidy way to launch Operation Swoop."

"In response to stimulated public opinion, we will arrest all the leading human right activists nationwide. We will detain them and keep them out of action for several months. We will invade their offices."

"I hope we will get some good computers and air conditioners from the raid. The air conditioner in this room isn't working and the head of administration has ignored all our memos…"

"Is that why you are getting so creative?"

"Don't you think we should enjoy some of the goodies they get from their foreign sponsors? We will declare that the arrested activists are dangerous suspects, and say we carted away their computers and office equipment because we want to conduct a through search for the murderers of Lawyer Kunle. We shall get police detectives to say that the computers hard disks are relevant to the investigation and that the air conditioners' compressors may have useful coded information inscribed on them."

"Super!"

"And remember to move a television set into the bastard's cell. Let's give him the freedom to watch 'Operation Swoop' on T.V."

Aluta

She saw what could be seen of him, his toe nails black and hard, toughed by the dust of his many wanderings. He was wrapped in bed-sheets and carried heavily. His friends struggled not to let him fall. Their fingers could barely get a grip on his body. His bones were broken like a twig cut into pieces. Beneath their grip, his body moved like an eel, like melting jelly, soft and deteriorating.

The students were clustered on the balcony in front of their rooms, looking on and dissecting the incident. The cashew trees blew gently in the wind. The hedge of plants glittered green, cigarette smoke rose from the boys and a strong urine stench from the grass at the back of the hostel. The gagging acidity stung her eyes with the fury of onions. The hum of voices roared in her ears.

Gently, they laid him inside the ambulance. Two of his friends jumped in with him and the blue siren began to wail. She pushed her way through the babbling crowd, past the Kanabe hall buttery and reading rooms, past the cafeteria tables still laden with cold, half-eaten beans and yams, until she was standing at the door of the Students' Union President.

She rapped on the door and a gruff voice bid her come in. She went in. The Students' Union President was propped up on pillows on his bed reading a novel by Harold Robbins and shoving spoonfuls of rice into his mouth. He stood up as she entered and pulled a seat for her.

"I would have invited you to join my meal but I know you will throw it up. What is wrong, Dr Linda? You look like you have been visited by a ghost."

"How can you call yourself Students' Union President and not know what is going on? Can't you hear the uproar all around you? You lie on your bed shoving rice into your mouth while a student was nearly murdered right in your own hall."

"O that? It's a war between the baboons and the monkeys. It's an animal fight. Human beings shouldn't get embroiled in it."

"Cut out the sarcasm. What is going on here?"

"Madame hall matron, it's a cult war between the Black Axe and the Knife Star."

"Gosh! A cult war! The boy was literally broken into pieces. I doubt if he will make the night."

"The boy is the district leader of the Knife Star. Save your worry. He is not as innocent as he looks. The Black Axe attacked him in revenge because his group launched a surprise offensive against them at their recent initiation ceremony and caused the death of one of their new members."

"What! Why wasn't this brought to the knowledge of the college authorities?"

"Dr Linda, in the real world, when men fight, real men don't go running home to their mamas. We are talking campus war here. Students' Mafia. The student that reportedly died of an asthmatic attack two weeks ago was in the Black Axe. The Knife Star stormed their hide-out and began attacking them with knifes, stones, horse whips and their leaders shot guns in the air."

"On campus?"

"It shouldn't amaze you. Great wars are fought on campus. And if you don't want to get into trouble, there are certain basic rules that must be obeyed. Tony broke one of the cardinal ones. He tried to take the girlfriend of the Black Axe chieftain. I think he got power drunk. The girl refused him and reported to her Black Axe boyfriend, who got his boys to give Tony a friendly warning. They beat up his security officer and sent a two word message to him —'Back off!'"

"I can't believe this. Your story sounds too fantastic. All these boys look so gentle and friendly."

"And very deadly, Dr Linda, very deadly. Anyway, Tony felt insulted and decided to lunch an attack. He surprised the Black Axe just as they were at the climax of their initiation ceremony, when their newly initiated members were supposed to drink the bowl of water mingled with drops of their own blood and their new brothers. When Tony and his boys breezed in, the boy who was drinking from the bowl of water and blood panicked in fright and choked. This brought on an asthmatic attack. Sadly he didn't have his medicine on him. Black Axe swore a terrible vengeance and bided time. When all was set, they trailed Tony to his palace."

"Palace?"

"Madame, every chieftain has a palace, a room where he holds court on campus. There he is consorted, consulted and pampered. The Black Axe lookouts made sure the Knife Stars security boys on duty that day were guys they could easily handle and then, they gave the signal. Seven hefty Black Axers stormed Tony's palace. His security boys and his girlfriends ran for their lives while they gave Tony the jelly cake."

"The bone-breaking beating they gave him?"

"Yes, ma'am, you are catching on fast…Tony's girlfriend and his security boys alerted some students. The Black Axers ran when irate students stormed the room but five of them were caught."

"Where are they now?"

"They have been handed over to the campus security policemen."

The roar of voices outside gradually rose to a crescendo. She peeped outside and saw the students furiously cutting off tree branches and brandishing them above their heads like weapons.

They were chanting their war-cry "we no go gree o, we no go gree, Great OTI, we no go gree."

She turned to the Students' Union President, her heart sinking, her hands grimly clutching the table by the bed. Her black eyes met his dark brown eyes.

He calmly told her, "Madam, we have a crisis on our hands."

The students began to pound on the door, "Presido, come out! Presido, come out! We want action! aluta continua!

Enough is enough! No more campus cults!"

He opened the door and walked out. The hall matron followed him.

The students continued their din. "We want action! We want action! We want action!"

Trying to soothe their brimming anger, he said "Great OTI, Coolu Temper!"

The students replied with a resounding "Noooo!"

"Great OTI, Coolu Temper!"

"Nooooh!"

The hall matron motioned to the crowd, shouting at the top of her voice, "The university authorities are aware of the unfortunate incident. The matter is being looked into. A panel shall be set up and all guilty offenders shall be prosecuted!"

The students roared "Noooo!... We want action! Instant action! We want action!"

Valiantly, she continued. "Please let the law take its course. The university authorities shall resolve the matter in the shortest possible time."

Some students bent down and hoisted the Student's Union President on their shoulders. Someone put a tree branch into his hand and they surged out like a sea wave, spilling all over the campus.

The hall matron turned back into the room. She shut the door, threw in the bolt and closed the windows. Like a caged lioness robbed of her cubs, she paced through the room, hearing the noise of breaking glass and bottles, hoping there would be no loss of life and fearing that her car parked in the hostel's parking lot would not be spared.

... Sensing a calm after the storm, after a time that seemed like forever, she opened the windows, a burst of fresh air poured in, refreshing her and bringing with it, the subdued voices of students. She opened the door and saw a girl struggling with her heavy suitcase. She asked her, "why are you moving your things?"

"The university has been closed," the girl replied. "The students went to the Vice-Chancellor's lodge. They broke down his gate and trampled his flower hedge. They locked the vice-chancellor and his family in the toilet. They raided his kitchen and broke valuables in his home. The registrar phoned the military governor who sent in a detachment of soldiers to stop the student's riot."

"O, my God!"

"The soldiers came like avenging maniacs, firing tear gas at the students. The students mobilized and drenched their handkerchief with kerosine to neutralize the effects of the tear-gas. They picked up unexploded tear-gas grenades and threw them back at the soldiers. And then, the soldiers opened fire into the crowd. Fiendishly, the bullets tore into the students. Pandemonium took over. Students fell like hail stones on the ground, fleeing in all directions. Screams and cries, tears and blood. It was horrifying. How could soldiers shoot defenseless students armed only with sticks and courage?"

For some moments, Dr Linda wearily lean against the door post and shut her eyes. Then, she slowly shut the door behind her and began walking towards the car park, past the cafeteria, still burdened with dirty plates, past the reading room, the Kanabe hall buttery, walking to her car...

She sees something iron and tapered laying on the grass. She looks closely. She sees what it is. She picks up the bullet.

The Leaking Bride

Yelema happened to be outside her family's compound that day when Papa Waire rode into her home on his Raleigh bicycle, his wrapper flapping in the wind and a big smile plastered on his face. She knelt down to greet him and her kid brothers clustered round the bicycle, admiring the multicoloured balls strung on the spokes of the wheel and the tassels on the handle bars. Deftly dropping the bicycle's brakes, Papa Waire stepped down, touched Yelema's shoulders affectionately and strode inside to see her father.

"Yelema, Yelema, go and bring the palmwine, the one I kept under the foot of the bed," she heard her mother calling to her. She ran in and fetched the gourd of palmwine and two tin cups from her mother's special set. She set them down before the men. Her father and Papa Waire beamed affectionately at their. She poured the wine into their cups and left the room…

Going into the kitchen she dragged the iron axe outside and began to cut wood for the next day. Her brother, Onome came running to her.

"Yelema, you are going to get married next week. I just heard Papa and Papa Waire talking about it. You are going to get married. Papa Waire wants to marry you." One of the wood chips hit him on the nose, as he hopped about excitedly.

Yelema dropped the axe and went to her mother, busily stirring soup on the fire: "Mama, Mama, Onome says he heard Papa say I will marry Papa Waire, next week – it is true?"

Her mother glanced at her and turned her attention to the contents she was stirring in the pot, speaking slowly, her voice keeping rhythm with the motions of stirrings:

"It is true, my daughter. I was going to tell you tonight. It is news that should bring you much joy. Papa Waire is a good man. He has a large rubber farm and a concrete block house. You will not lack for anything, he will look after you."

"But Mama, most of his children are older than me! He even has several grandchildren. He is an old man."

"My daughter, you are no longer a child. You are now a woman. You started seeing your blood five months ago. It is time for you to get married and Papa Waire is a good suitor. He will be kind to you and he will treat you well, like his own child."

She turned on her heels, going to sit under the banana tree at the back of the kitchen. The birds nested on the tree flew off as she approached. She heard something rustle among the fallen banana leaves, perhaps it was a snake but she was too confused to be afraid. Deftly folding her little wrapper between her legs, she sat down and began to think…

She was big, big for her age. She had just turned twelve. She was too big, it seemed for her father's house, perhaps that was why they wanted to marry her off. At the time when her mates were still running round bare chested, she had began to pull up her wrapper over her chest to cover her budding breasts. She had the beginnings of a wide hip which her mother told her was very good for child bearing. Taking a little twig to clean her toe nails, she tried to confront her fear but she was too much of a child, she could not construct the proper questions, the possible options she had.

She tried to think of what it would mean to be a wife. She could only think of cooking and washing and cleaning and a man sticking something into you at night. She did not know what was stuck into wives at night, she had only overhead her auntie, Mama Porgi, complaining to her mother that her husband wanted to stick it into her every night. She knew wives cooked and cleaned and had babies because her mother and her stepmother, cooked and cleaned and had babies.

Cleaning her fingernails, she knew that she would no longer play with her mates on the village lanes in the glow of the full moon. She began to think of Papa Waire. She admired his bicycle, it was shiny new and the balls on the spoke rolled in a galaxy of colours every time he rode past at top speed. But she was afraid of marrying him. He was an old man. He always smiled kindly at her but old people died. What if he died soon? And what would she do if he tied to stick his thing into her?

"Yelema, Yelema, come out of the banana grove!" Her mother knew that was her hiding place. "Come out and take your father's food to him.". ..

Her mother, gazing at her daughter as she bent down to pick the tray of her father's meal, was not unsympathetic to her feelings. She understood her fear because her own father had also married her off at an early age, but she felt her daughter was luckier with her lot. She would be getting married to a much older man, a man who had a good reputation for his kindness and generosity. His two other wives were quite old too. They would all treat her like their daughter, not a rival for their husband's attention.

She had married her own husband, Yelema's father, when he was a hot-headed man in his thirties and the early years of the marriage had been turbulent. He liked to drink and when he got drunk, he would come home and punch her. There was never enough money for food from his night watchman's job at the government village health centre and since he spent nearly most days sleeping off his hangovers, very little food came from his farm for the family. Each of his wives had to look after her own children.

She had to work very hard, waking up early, trekking miles on the damp dew-laden paths to the few rubber trees she inherited from her father. She would check each tin cup tied to its tree, carefully pouring the white latex juice bled by the trees during the night into an iron pail. She would balance the bucket on her head, careful not to spill a drop of liquid as she hurried home. Once home, she would pour the juice into the iron mould at the back of the house and leave it to harden in the sun. Then she would light a wood fire and begin to fry wet cassava flour in her wide iron pan. Once a fortnight, she would sell her rubber sheets to the produce buyer from a Warri company and every market day, she sold her roasted cassava flour and the smoked fish she traveled once a month to buy at Okere market.

Her husband's senior wife never ceased to shout in the yard, gossiping with her friends and parading her five sons. She had only two. Two sons and three daughters. Some youth corps members who worked for the government, teaching and living in the school opposite her home had come three months ago, preaching family planning to her. They had come to buy some roasted peanuts when she suddenly had a fit of vomiting. After scattering in different directions, they came back cautiously.

"Mama Yelema, what is the matter?"

"Do sit down, have you been to see the doctor?"

"I no sick, I only get belle."

"But you already have five children."

"You work so hard, trying to feed your children. You are putting a strain on yourself. You should have gone to the nurse at the health centre for some family planning advice."

"Which kin family planning? You wan make dem tie my belle? My pickin never reach."

"Mama Yelema!"

"I beg make una leave me o, any bodi wey say make I no born more pickin, me and him go fight!"

Seeing her aggressive stance, they had quietly withdrawn. How could she make them see that sons were vital tools on the negotiating table of marriage? The more sons she had, the more her security and her standing in her home and in the village. Daughters were married off. You only added them to someone else's family but sons were yours, the keepers of their father's homestead, the stamp of their mothers' presence, banana shoots replacing the old tree when it died. She needed more sons. In her silent duel with the senior wife for influence in her husband's family, the more sons she had, the more victory would tilt her way.

That night, when her daughter was undressing for bed, she had patted her on the back and said, "Don't worry, just be a good girl, you will get used to the marriage." Yelema did not know what to say. There were questions in her mind but children were not supposed to query their parents. She laid on her mat and tried to sleep.

* * *

She had sores between her legs which made walking difficult. She wobbled, tilting to one side, shifting nearly all her weight onto her right leg. One night, three weeks ago, Papa Waire had come with members of his family to her father house. They came with some gourds of palmwine and some money in an envelope.

And Papa Waire had taken her to his home as his wife. That night, when he stuck his thing into her, she had cried out at the searing pain. He did not stop. And she could hear his two older wives giggling in the next room. She cried at the sight of her blood which seemed to make him proud. Two days ago, she noticed she had started dripping urine. She ran to the pit latrine, clenching all her muscles, trying to force out all the urine in her. Still she dripped urine throughout the day. She stuffed her body with rags and tried to surround herself with the antiseptic smell of onions and garlic. She saw the older wives sniff at the air suspiciously. She wanted to run home to her mother.

As she bent to give water to her husband, his oldest son living in the city who had just come home to visit his father stared at her and asked "Are you alright?"

Her husband, proudly showing off the still visible henna 'bridegroom' designs on his hands and feet to his son, touched her thigh and said to his son, "dis na my new wife."

The Fowler's Snare

"Gbemi, you do not need that ridiculous headgear. We are not going to see the president. We are only going to an Ijebu party."

"The more reason why I need to get my headtie just right. The Ijebus are famous for their parties."

Peering into her dressing table mirror and lining her eyes with Kohl, she continued. "I hear they save up in anticipation of a party, just to be sure no occasion to celebrate is ever bereft of money for food, drinks and clothes."

Her husband laughed. "You shouldn't be listening to such gossip. Anyway, Tayo has always been a modest guy. I don't think he would indulge in such excess."

"You can never tell with an Ijebu man…"

"Madam, you look good enough. We are running late. Can we now leave?"

He came to the mirror and drew her away, nearly unsettling her headtie in the process. They walked out to the car and as she drew open the door of the backseat, he said, "I am driving".

She looked at him in surprise, "But you haven't driven in a very long time. You said you no longer wished to drive yourself since we got the driver. Where is he?"

"I gave him the day off. Get in the car and let's go. Don't worry. You can still trust my driving."

She slid in beside him on the front seat, fastening her seat belt… The red earth baked in the hot sun on both sides of the road. Cars sped past. The siren of a Federal Road Safety Corps car sang nosily in the hot morning, chasing after some speeding vehicles. A second Corps vehicle moved ahead on the traffic lane and began to lead the other cars in a convoy.

"These guys are going to make us late."

"It is better late than never. They are only controlling the mad speed of the cars. This road has become a death trap. Last

Christmas, twenty people plunged into the river when their over speeding bus somersaulted on the bridge we've just passed. Anyway, it is a party. It really doesn't matter when we get there."

"Tayo is a stickler for time. I promised him we shall be there by twelve noon."

"That time is rather unusual. Most week end parties usually start at four p.m. Are you sure you got the time right?"

"I am positive…"

The perfume of wild flowers thickened in the air. White egrets and hawks rose from their rocky perches fluttering their wings on the waves of the wind. Mothers slung babies on their backs, as they trekked to their farms. Village women selling fresh farm produce by the road shielded themselves from the sun under the sturdy tree branches. Cars pulled up by the side of the road to buy red tomatoes, brown yams, white cassava flour, yellow pineapples, green bananas, clusters of cream-coloured and deep purple onions. The landscape looked like a master piece artwork come to life.

Emeka turned off the highway onto a dusty road track, driving into a forest. Slowly, he began to manoeuver the car over the bumps, trying to avoid the gaping holes where erosion had eaten into the road.

"Are you sure we are on the right track?, Haven't we missed the way?"

"I am positive."

The car bumped and jarred. She could hear the tea she drank that morning sloshing round in her stomach.

"Emeka, we really need to change the shock absorbers of this car. My headgear is nearly falling off. I don't know how these Ijebu people can spend so much money on parties and leave the road leading to their town in such a terrible state."

Emeka said nothing. The lane got narrower and narrower. The tall grass and shrubs on the sides of the road began to brush against the car. Weeds were rattling beneath the car. She could feel the scratching under her seat. She wound up the car window and turned in exasperation to Emeka, "Are we on the right road?"

"Will you shut up and let me concentrate?"

"You brought me into the middle of nowhere for one funny Ijebu man's party and you don't want me to ask questions?"

Emeka ignored her. Soon, they came out into a little circular clearing in the middle of the forest and stopped in front of a mud hut. Emeka stopped the car, removed the key from the ignition and instinctively handed it over to her. He wound up the window at his side and said "Get out, madam, we have arrived."

She looked round. She could only see the bees buzzing in the sun and the mud hut standing at the edge of the clearing. No chairs, no tables, no canopies, no smell of cooking in the air, and no other human being except her husband and her.

"Emeka, is this the venue of the party? Why is everywhere so quiet? Where is everybody? Is this your friend's house? There is no sign of a party out here."

"Madam, instead of sitting in there and asking me questions, why don't you come out and find answers for yourself."

He got out of the car, slammed the door on his side, walked to the back of the car and began to drum his fingers impatiently on the bonnet, waiting for her to come out. She came out, straightening her headgear. She sniffed at the air in vain, trying to catch the whiff of jollof rice and fried meat. She stood for some moments, flexing her toes in her high-heeded sandals and walked to the back of the car.

Her husband smiled at her and ushered her towards the mud hut. The hut rectangular in shape had chalk lines drawn all over its walls, horizontally. It looked well kept. The frontage had just been swept. Walking towards the hut, she could see the zigzag patterns the broom had made in the red earth. The ground around the wall looked like it had been carefully weeded by hand. The silence made her uneasy. Nobody came out of the hut. Her husband opened the door of the hut and lightly propelled her inside.

Darkness enveloped her as she stepped inside. The hut was gloomy. If there were windows, there were no signs of them. Coming from the glare outside, the darkness blinded her. As her eyes got used to the darkness, she saw two shadowy figures sitting in two large armchairs in the middle of the room. The two figures stirred when her husband shut the door behind them.

Two voices said "Welcome!", one, the voice of an old man, rather hoarse with age. The second sounded like a middle-aged woman. The old man's voice repeated, "Welcome my son. We have been expecting you."

Her husband replied, "I am sorry Baba, there was some traffic jam on the way."

Nobody offered her a seat. And there certainly was no sign of a party. The room was eerily quiet. Only a oil lamp glowed in the darkness. The room had a long bench leaning against the wall, facing the old man and the woman. The woman was dressed in a green-patterned blouse and wrapper. She had on a cowrie necklace. The old man was bare chested, a thick white hand woven cloth covered his lower body. He also wore a necklace and anklets of cowries. The man and the woman kept on starring at her. Their stares made her knees shake.

She turned to her husband, wanting to tell him to take her out of there immediately but her tongue would not obey her. She opened her mouth but it snapped shut in a vice-grip as if someone had thrown a magnet between her lips. She saw the old man and old woman were still staring at her.

Her husband was on his knees before the old man. She decided to seat on the bench. As she sat down, she suddenly felt something warm, liquid and slippery gush between her thighs. It could not be her menstrual period, she thought. She had just finished her menses, two weeks ago and her twenty-eight day cycle was as regular as dawn. She fervently hoped it was not her period. Yet she knew it was. It always heralded its arrival in the same manner. Something warm, liquid and slippery gushing between her thighs: Fretting that it had caught her completely off-guard with no hygienic towels or tissue paper or tampons, she feared that her cream–coloured buba and iro would be stained.

Just as she was about to stand up to furtively check her wrapper, the old man suddenly snapped at her husband.

"Why did you bring her?"

"Baba, she is perfect for our purpose. I described her to you and you said she would be perfect for the ritual. She is a close relative. She is my wife."

"Yes, my son, I know she is your wife but she is bleeding. The way of women is upon her. She is bleeding. We cannot use her. You have completely wasted my time. The last time you were here, I specifically told you not to bring a woman doing her monthly thing. The medicine will not work. Everything will be completely neutralized."

"Baba, she is not bleeding, I know her cycle. She is my wife, she finished her menses about two weeks ago."

"Do you dare to contradict me, child? I have been making wealth medicine for people for years. I do not need to undress her. I know a bleeding woman when I see one."

Like a heavy branch falling on the earth with a thud, it dawned on her that her husband had brought her here to be sacrificed. Whirling at her, in the same instant, was the knowledge that she had the car keys on her. Her brain calculated feverishly. She looked at her husband and the couple. Both men were still arguing. Slowly, she slid off her high-heeled sandals. She sprang to her feet, sprinting for the door.

Frantically, her nails clawed on the wood, she turned the door knob, swung the door open and jumped outside. She raced to the car. She nervously groped for the door keyhole with sweaty palms. From the corner of her eyes, she saw Emeka coming after her, her death clearly written on his face. She got the door open, slammed it shut, locked it centrally and fumbled for the ignition. Emeka reached the car and tugged at the door on her side. The lock held. He pounded on the window. The glass smashed. As he lunged for her throat, she swerved her neck, turning the ignition at the same moment. The car roared with rage, leaping forward onto the narrow trail.

Turn Table

As far as her eyes can see, the village is redolent with green leaves. The birds are chirping their good morning to the sun. The grasshoppers are fluttering on the paths and there is an excitement in her. Today, her week of love begins. There is a spring in her footsteps as she walks to the well to fetch water for her bath. On her way back from the well, she meets her husband's first wife's daughter, Temilola who kneels down to greet her.

"Get up, my husband." Iyawo replied, "Good morning, the beautiful one who glistens like shea butter. Did you sleep well? How are your younger brothers?"

"Iyawo, we are well. Let me help you with your bucket."

"Thank you, my husband."

Her husband's children were also respectfully addressed as 'my husband.' She hands over the bucket to Temilola. Temilola deftly balances the bucket on her head and heads for the family bathroom where she places it on the wooden floor. Iyawo steps into the bathroom, a circular shelter built with sturdy wooden planks, just a few yards away from the main house She pulls the door shut and loosens her wrapper. She plays with her waist beads, admiring her hour-glass figure.

The excitement courses through her again. Today, her week of love begins. She pours the cold water on her body, every nerve in her is tingling as she begins to soap her body with the black soap. The extra money she paid for the Ijebu black soap was well worth it. It had a very rich lather. Nobody else made black soap as well as Ijebu women. They added extra moisturizing and cleansing ingredients like camwood, honey, blue stones and spices. Their women were famous for their shinny, smooth skin.

Rinsing herself completely clean, Iyawo wears her wrapper…Entering her room, she oils herself with coconut oil and lines her eyes with antimony. She hurries her breakfast of corngruel and leftover vegetable soup. She has told Modele to expect her when the sun grew hot. She is to make a special week of love hairstyle.

Modele, the hairdresser, is already waiting for her when she arrives:

"Good morning my friend. Everyone can easily guess that you are in your week of love, there is a real spring in your steps."

"Modele, I am sure you understand how it is. You know my husband has four wives, it makes the queue a lot longer."

As they sit plaiting her hair, passers-by greet them.

"You are making a thing of beauty." The women teases Iyawo. "This must be your week of love."

Iyawo hurries to the market, walking a little taller, preening to show off her new hair style. She also has to cook for her husband because it is her turn to sleep with him for a week. And nothing must go wrong. She cannot afford it.

Adeola, her husband likes his food very much, and any wife who is late with her cooking gets a very expensive punishment. She remembers the price Mama Ronke, his second wife, paid when she was late with their husband's food two months ago. Their husband had arrived with two friends for lunch and when he found out that the food was still on the fire, he calmly called Ronke and told her,

"Go to Mama Peju's buka down the road. Tell her I want ten wraps of pounded yam, eight cuts of bush meat, four pieces of smoked fish, four pieces of cow leg and a large gourd of palm wine and tell her to change it to your mother's account."

Ronke felt like fainting on the spot. She knew it meant they would not have the new clothes her mother had promised her and her younger brothers and sisters for the harvest festival. But she dared not say a word to her father. She hurried to obey. Her mother, overhearing in the backyard kitchen, where she was blowing hard on the wood fire, burst into tears. The food her husband ordered would wipe out all the money she had saved from selling some of her farm produce, the money she painstakingly kept aside after every big market day, to buy things for herself and her children and to supplement the house-keeping allowance her husband gave each wife when it was her turn to cook for the family. The other wives could only console her but there was nothing they could do to change their husband's decree…

Iyawo finishes early and dishes the food into her most expensive set of earth ware plates kept for special times like this. She wraps the pounded yam in a beautiful aso-oke cloth to keep it warm. She arranges the food on a clean wooden tray and wears a scarf on her hair. She walks to the table in the empty living room and kneels before it. She carefully places the food on the table. Her only audience, the heavy mahogany furniture, the wooden window shutters and the silence echoing in her ears. Why she kneels down to an empty room, she does not ask. This is the inheritance her mother passed on to her. That is how to put your husband's food on the table. She had been told. It is a husband's honour even though he is not there to see it. A knee salute to an absent lord.

Rising up, she begins to feel the juices of her body, the natural oils in her loins. She walks into his bedroom, unites her wrapper and carefully arranges her hair. She climbs into his bed, waiting for him to come to sleep and smiling at the memory of the two dogs she had seen locked together on her way from the market.

* * *

Adeola is walking through the meandering streets, lost in his thoughts and the comforting fragrance of goat dung. He nearly collides with a man riding a bicycle.

The cyclist screams at him. "Please watch your steps. Do

not bring your bad-luck to me."

Adeola ignores him completely. He is too busy plotting. How on earth was he going to manage with two women tonight?

He knew he had to be really creative about it. Iyawo must not find out about his concubine, Olabisi. If she did, she would refuse to make love with him tonight. How was he going to sneak Olabisi into his house? Iyawo would now be lying on his bed, waiting for him, his pounded yam, warm and awaiting his pleasure but he did not wish to cancel his rendezvous with Olabisi. Her parents were so strict. Their tryst for tonight had taken three weeks of strategic planning. Ha. What can a man do? He will use his prerogative as a husband. He will bring her boldly into his home and ask his third wife, Olanike, to prepare some food for her and prepare the guest room, the room usually reserved for his friends when they came visiting.

Olanike will grumble under her breath but she will not query him. After handing Olabisi to Olanike, he will have his dinner, make love to Iyawo and caress her to sleep and then, he will dash off to Olabisi. Having sorted out his worries, Adeola hurries his steps, knowing it is a good thing he decided to wear his big, flowing agbada. It turns out to be a perfect camouflage for his erection. If he had worn the white man's shirt and trousers, every passer-by would have known he was on his way to a romp.

... Adeola breaks into a big smile, thinking of Olabisi, already waiting for him under the cottonseed tree.

...Adeola rolls off Iyawo. She breathes a sigh of contentment.

...Adeola draws her into the crook of his arm, wanting to caress her to sleep so he could quickly go to Olabisi, impatiently waiting for him in the guest room. Iyawo giggles:

"My dear husband, I need to rush to the toilet, I will be right back."

"Do hurry, you know it is such a good night..."

They both laugh as she wraps her wrapper round her

body and walks out. She quietly opens the door leading into the backyard. She does not want to wake any of her co-wives. Stepping on the soft, sandy ground, she breathes deeply. She threads gently on the ground, on this first night of her week of sleep. She hopes the dog will recognize her as a friend, a member of the family and not bark. Looking left and right and gazing into the silence around her, she sneaks into the bush behind the bathroom where she had hidden her most precious things...

Against her will, her father had given her as wife to Adeola because he owed Adeola a large sum of money he could not afford to pay back. Adeola had shown his interest in her though he already had three wives. He told her father he could convert the debt into dowry if her father gave her to him as wife. Her father agreed. She had pleaded and wept but had no other choice, since her other suitor, Akinomo, who she deeply loved, was too poor to pay her father's debt. She had bided her time, seeing Akinomo secretly and sending him presents of food through discreet children.

And recently, Akinomo had come into a good inheritance. His father had died and his share of his father's property was a small cocoa farm. The last harvest had been very good. Akinomo could now afford to pay back the dowry Adeola paid on her. Her father's debt to him.

Lifting her face into the wind, she whistles the agreed signal, three owl cries. The reply floats to her on the night, sounding like swine foraging in the village rubbish dump. Deftly, she balances her basket on her head and walks in the direction of the swine grunts. The full moon lights her path. The frogs are croaking a mating song. She strides without fear on this freedom night. She navigates her path with bare hands, parting the tangled plants, her gaze locks on the large cashew tree at the end of the bush, under which Akinomo awaits her.

In her joy, her eyes disdain the ground and so, she steps on something that sprang like a cougar and sank its teeth deep in her ankle. Her scream slaps the face of night as she falls like a bundle of firewood, carelessly thrown on the earth, her basket tumbles into the undergrowth, spewing out her clothes, beads and pots. "Help! Help me! Help! This is death! Help!".

Her cries uncork a cacophony of response. Dogs growl and bark. Sleeping crickets awaken, chirping a consolatory anthem. Akinomo, hearing his lover's screams, urges his legs to run, run, run-away, guessing she must have been bitten by a viper whose bite was always nearly fatal. What else could have made her bawling so strident? He had money to marry a wife, not bury a dead lover. The eyes that must see no evil needs legs with the speed of winds.

Adeola, languidly awaiting Iyawo's return, hears a woman's criesl. He leaps out of bed and hurriedly lights an oil lamp. He wraps a cloth around his body, securing the knot behind his neck. He lifts up the oil lamp as he opens the door to find an enraged Olabisi, who had come in search of him.

White Darling

All of a sudden, I look into the rear-view mirror, I see her sauntering in my direction…my goodness, there was no way I could maneuver the car out of the traffic jam. The two-lane road had become four lanes. I take a quick look round to see how I could possibly disguise myself in a minute. I remove my baseball cap from the back seat of the car and jam it on my head. I pull my black sunglasses from the glove-box and slip them on. I furiously wound up all the car windows and press the doors auto lock. I sit squirming in my seat. I watch as she slowly walks past my car, my chest gradually relaxing like a balloon grudgingly letting out air. She is dressed in an old, faded jeans jacket and trousers. The jacket is torn under the arms and the elbows are frayed. Her grimy tennis shoes, once bright red, now looks like old, dried blood.

Images of our last encounter floats before my eyes. My client, Nkechi, had wanted a two-bedroom apartment in Surulere. She did not like any of the ones I had shown her. Sometimes, I really hated being an estate agent. It was so difficult, finding the right apartments and most of my clients treat me with disdain. They turn up their noses, speaking English with fake British accents and telling stories of how someone they know lost money to an estate agent. Don't they know that there are pigs in every profession?

I found an apartment I thought Nkechi would like. The landlord said his son was living in it until the end of the week but we could come and have a look. Nkechi works till quite late, she works in a bank and we could only go to check out the apartment at nine p.m. We looked at the apartment, Nkechi loved it and the landlord's son was very warm. He invited us to join him for a drink. Just as we were declining the invitation, saying we had to run, we suddenly heard the violent rustling of the bead curtain in the living room. Nkechi screamed as a woman, stark naked, ran towards her. I grabbed Nkechi and we ran to the door. The naked woman ran after us and caught Nkechi by the waist, pulling at her shorts.

The landlord's son was too stunned for a few seconds to react. I pulled Nkechi free and pushed her outside. I turned round to grip the woman, giving Nkechi more time to get away. The landlord's son helped me wrestle her to the ground. It seemed she had the strength of ten men. Trussing her on the floor, with anger and fear, I shouted to the landlord's son. "Who is this mad woman?"

With tears tricking down his face, he replied quietly, "She is my friend, her name is Bimbo."

We bundled her into a room and jammed the door shut. I left the house with her screamed obscenities echoing in my ears. Nkechi never forgave me, for what she called the fright of her life. I lost my client. I lost a good house commission.

He thinks he is smart… He thinks I did not see him. I have the gift of sight and I know how to use it. Even in the darkest places, I see clearly. They think I am an idiot. They say I am a fool… That night, they kicked me all over and bundled me like a bag of dirty clothes, throwing me into that dark room and locking me in. But I was only teasing the woman. I don't know why she screamed. It was only a game. …I just decided to ignore him, I really don't need money now. Yekini paid well for Daddy's tyres. Poor mummy. I know he would have screamed at her, "Your daughter has stolen my tyres!"

My father shouldn't label me . I am just a woman in love. A woman who fell in love with a needle and warm, white liquid bubbling in the spoon. Why does he find it so hard to understand?. After all, this is a free world. I have never begrudged him his several girl friends. I never ever told my mother about them. She knows of course. She found out a long time ago. She once confronted one openly at a family friend's wedding, I thought I would die of embarrassment…

In a house surrounded by tall palm trees on the shores of the Lagos lagoon, on a night of music and gyrating bodies, I met my white darling. It was the soul of the party. The music rose into the night air, cuddling the stars. I was young and thirsty for life and all the experience that could come my way. I did not hesitate. Sam, a classmate, noticing how quickly l fell in love with the needle and the white powder, whispered to me.

"You know, if you want, this crack could fetch you a lot of money"

"How?"

"I hear you are a very good actress. With an actress, all things are possible because you can choose your script and direct your own production."

"I don't understand?"

"Ever couriered before? Are you brave enough?

I was high that night. I truly believed that all things were possible. Sam took me to Paul, the American co-ordinator of the drug ring who used the country as their transit camp. Paul helped me explore my potential as an actress. A perfect director, he was the one who suggested that the handicapped act would be the most convincing to carry off. Who would easily suspect a handicapped lady in a wheel chair going abroad for treatment? Who would suspect that her wheelchair had heroin carefully concealed in it? After we had rehearsed and were ready to premiere the performance, I simply sneaked out of home one morning, telling my parents that I was going across the border to Cotonou for a day's visit with a friend. Two days later, I called my mother from the United States of America just to let her know I was okay and she need not worry.

I was deaf to her pleas and her cries. I could hear the haunting flute of my white darling calling me, come, come, come. For three years, home became an horizon across the sea beckoning but the ocean was in between. I couldn't resist the money, the adventure, the power, the glamour. Until the morning the curtain closed on my act and there was no applause inviting me for a second bow. The police raided my apartment.

A kind neighbour who met me going home warned me: "The cops are on your tail. Go and cool your heels."

That day I really learnt to appreciate plastic. I took my plastic smart card, went to the automatic teller machine and withdraw all my cash. Disguised like an half-illiterate man whose English was so bad, that his mouth was better off closed, I fled the United States.

I, the prodigal daughter came home with no courage to return to my father's house. I lived in hotels, saving face and keeping up the charade of glamour until my money ran out. My darling became more possessive, demanding my life blood. I had to have more and more of crack cocaine. The dealers became more ruthless. Men I had fed and nurtured said to me "Pay or perish." I paid with my clothes, with my jewelry and when I had no more, I paid with my body.

I would rise in the morning with disheveled hair, eyes squinting at the sun, toes peeping from my shoes, clothes hanging on me however they choose. I would trek the streets of Lagos, lurking at the bus stops, begging traders and passers by for money to eat, money which I would spend on my needles, my powder, my thirst.

In a city where people do not mind their own business, word soon reached my parents. My mother sought me out and took me home, weeping bitterly at the sight of scabies on my unwashed body. My father simply looked at me and walked out. While settling my dust encrusted behind into my parents' cream sofa, I heard my father drive out. He returned late that night to scream at my mother, berating her for disgracing him with a daughter like me. That night, at the hour when only owls are awake, I climbed out of the window and returned to the streets.

This is why I make the streets my home. To protect my mother. She keeps looking for me on the street corners and in sleazy bars. She keeps getting my uncles and aunties to clean me up and bring me home. But how can I leave my needles desolate, the cigarette lighter boiling the lovely juice in the spoon? The white powder reaching for a hug, saying; keep me flowing in your veins.

I really cannot understand my father. He has always tended to over-react. After all, I have only stolen a few of his car tyres, car radio and mirrors and his gold tie clip. Ha, he should ask my mother…I hate to steal her things but it cannot be helped. I only stole her gold jewelry box after I had sold all my own things. I even tried to sell my university degrees certificates. They are no use to me but nobody wanted them. It is really a hard life.

Someone should tell my mother not to worry about me. I have tried to die but I lived to see another day. So, I suppose I am going to be okay. One night when everyone had gone to bed, I went into the kitchen and took a sharp kitchen knife, the one the steward often used to cut up chicken for dinner. I went back to my room and laid on my bed. I held the knife to my throat, turning my neck to the exact angle I imagined my jugular vein would be. But in my mind's eye, I suddenly saw my red blood sprayed on the cream-coloured walls of my bedroom. Just like chicken blood. Huh, I did not want my blood sprayed on the earth so ordinarily. I am not really keen on bloody graffiti. Besides how could Mummy bear to clean my blood from the wall? I know the housemaid would rather lose her job than clean after a suicide. I held a serious conference with myself deciding. I should go in a more dignified way or, perhaps, I am really chicken.

I also tried a gun once but Mummy came knocking on my door just at the moment I put the gun to my head. I quickly hid it under the mattress. The moment passed. I am alive not because I tried to live. I just have not succeeded at dying. Since I couldn't die, I just swallow whatever lemon I am tossed each day. Crying when I am hungry for love, smiling when I am in the embrace of my darling, sleeping under the bridges.

It is so freeing, so relaxing and there are always one or two cronies to have a party with. Three is never a crowd. We simply place three stones on the floor and stuff the middle with paper picked from the street. We light our stone and paper stove with a cigarette lighter and soon we have a burning delta for our sweetheart. Tunde first started the joke, he said our cooking contraption looked like a drawing of the Niger delta. He used to be a geology student...we sit round the needle, the sun hot on our faces or the moon bright and fluorescent on us, the cold night nearly feeling warm on our bodies. Day or night, my darling is such a cosy cloak.

The silly man. He thinks I did not recognize him...wearing black sunglasses and looking like a stupid actor... I need a quick embrace, I need to sit and rest somewhere. I think I will walk back and perch on his car bonnet and love my darling.

Crystal Woman

I first saw her walking on the wide, sandy village path. Her feet sank step by step, nearly ankle deep into the white sand, glistening like quartz jewels in the sun. The wind rustled her dress, blew it round her legs, whipping it, revealing glimpses of her petticoat.

In the distance, I could see the trees mourning on the banks of the river. Palm trees forever barren of fruits, their fronds broken like amputated limbs. Mangrove trees dark with oil slick. I had taken several walks down to the river and I have been astounded by its deadness. It looked dark, oily and dubious. The water sat still unmoving, clogged up by oil spillages by the petroleum companies prospecting in the area. Children, their bloated stomachs huge with disease and large hungry eyes swam the dark water, visiting their bamboo basket traps in hope of bitter fish.

Sometimes, on my morning walks, I met villagers, trudging back from harvesting their rubber tree farms. The sour sweet smell of rubber sap rose thick in the air about them. The women, haggard before their time, the swing in their hips long gone. Bent into subjection, laden down with teeming children to feed and a land, infertile, sucked lifeless. Only groundnuts flourished in the left over soil, whatever the bush rats left of them. The cassava plants waved sickly at the sun. The yam tubers came out of the earth, small, impoverished, like runt pigs born before their time.

In the market place, poverty startles like images from a back and white photograph album, no colourful array of vegetables and tubers, the stalls stood like pock marks on an adult face, solitary, a few trays of tomatoes, shriveled looking onions, soaked cowhide meat, fish dried into nearly stiff skeletons.

I had tried very hard to change my National Youth Service posting away from this disconsolate village. I had complained about the extra large mosquitoes, the appalling absence of everyday amenities, how I had to walk miles and miles before I got to the main road. All my pleas fell on unyielding rock. The officials insisted that I must go back to the village.

And so resigned to a year of intense boredom, I settled down to seduce the teenage school girls, the only abundant diversion the village offered until I saw her, the lady of the swirling skirt. What else would describe that thundering silence? Like the still of an industrial generator, quietening without warning.

Edosa Community Secondary School, where I had the chore of teaching year one students the English Language, had been invited to participate in a public schools debate and I was one of the teachers that led the Edosa delegation to the event. The debate had livened up. The Edosa boys were investing brawn and words, telling the crowd why fathers were more important than mothers, babbling away at the speed of a fast train...

* * *

I was standing at the edge of the crowd and beginning to lose interest in the proceedings, when I saw her strolling fluidly down the sandy path. Something deep inside me surged joyously and felt very afraid.

I started walking after her but as if she sensed my presence, she hurried her heels, digging them in and out of the sand. I felt the electricity of her flight. Flares after flares, after flares, like a power transmitter blowing its brains up. I ran, canceling all my rules with each step. I who always scoffed at chemistry had been caught by my shirt cuffs! I caught up with her at the village motor-park. I drew her by the hand and smiled,

"Why are you running away?"

"Life does not wait. I have got to keep up with it."

"Please, do not go, there is a power transmitter blowing up in me. You have made me electric."

"I do not believe in chemistry," she replied, her voice, the tinkling brooks of harmattan streams, "but I bear buckets of cold water."

"You want to kill me? Water and electricity breed fatal shocks."

"Do you not think that the earth is already over-populated?"

I had met my match. My arsenal of words had sorely let me down. I followed her quietly.

"…I, I do not know your name but you are as familiar to me as my sister's voice."

"I am Crystal, I light up the dark ages."

"Crystal , I am entrapped in your eyes."

She hissed and marched on. I ran ahead of her, did a triple somersault in the sand and landed in front of her face. A crowd of half-naked children, thinking they had been blessed with a free acrobatic show, began to gather. She burst into laughter. I noticed that her dimples were uncommonly deep.

"See, I have rolled in the dust at your feet. Will you not have mercy and talk a little with me?"

"Alright! Mr. Electric…"

We plopped down on a bench under a spreading umbrella tree. Time flowed on like mountain dust blown to the four winds, uncatchable. We talked in ebbs and flows, galloping with our words, wallowing in our histories. She was also in the National Youth Service Corp, a medical doctor doing her service two towns away from mine. How come I had not noticed her at the national orientation camp?

"Oh, we do not move in the same circles, I'm sure."

"What is that supposed to mean?"

"Well you look like you fraternize with the red crowd, wine, women, and vice…"

"…Aw, I am not so bad, I like to party a little, anyway, where were you on camp?"

"Guess, where would Crystal dwell?"

"With the Orange people, there her light will shine."

"You are off the mark. I don't like orange. "

"Em, em…"

"You could have found me if you came to church."

Inside me, the fire cools a little as I grapple with the revelation that I had fallen for a woman who loves church. She got up to go…

"I will be on call in an hour. I have got to go now."

I did not want to leave her.

"Please, let me come with you."

"What about the students you came with?"

"The Head teacher will take them back."

"In that case, do let the head teacher know you are coming with me."

"No, he will cook up an excuse to detain me."

"But be sure to write a note and let him know where you are."

As I scribbled a quick note, I notice one of my students trying to sneak past us.

"You! come here! Why are you hiding?"

"Sir, I was hungry… So I just hurried out to get some bread"

"Alright, make sure you give this note to Mr. Laskana. I am going somewhere. I will see you guys in school. Let us go."

A bus drove past. We stopped it and entered. As we neared her town, I was arrested by a message as gripping as a strait jacket. All my being beeped one message in clear consonants… '*Do not go any further.*' I tried to shake it off with a flick of my head but my body just became immobile. Panic crashed in.

"Having second thoughts?"

"No, but something is telling me not to go any further…"

"In that case, you had better obey."

I wished I could shake her out of her calm composure. She turned to the bus conductor and asked him to stop the driver. The bus stopped and I jumped down. She shook my hand and pressed something into it. I open my hand. It is a bar of chocolate.

"Will you not come with me?, I urge…."

"Have you forgotten that I am going on call in a few minutes?"

"I will come and see you tomorrow then."

"Suit yourself."

She smiled and waved at me as the bus zoomed off in a cloud of dust.

* * *

From somewhere in the centre of dreamland, I was irritated by the sound of wailing. It rose louder and louder. I battled to be free of it but it dragged me into wakefulness. My eyes fluttered open. The wailing rose in tempo just outside my room. I came out, wearing my white night shirt, barefoot in my hurry. As I dashed out, I saw Jude, my flat mate weeping on the pavement.

I ran toward him. He took one look at me, screamed and ran off. I ran after him, shouting "wait for me". I caught up with him at the principal's lodge. A crowd had already gathered. Above the din, some phrases rang out.

"No! No!, he cannot be dead."

"Our teacher cannot be dead."

"We still saw him yesterday at the debate."

Jude ran into the crowd, screaming. "Help me!, Help, it is his ghost." The students ran away. The teachers leapt on me, pinching and throwing sand on me. I was frantic, gulping for air and trying to keep the sand out of my eyes. Because I did not dissolve when they threw sand on me, they became convinced that l was no phantom. Then they explained:

"You sent a note to Mr. Laskana, saying you were travelling to Kaseh with a lady you met at the debate. Because it was all so sudden, the boy decided to jot down the plate number of the bus he saw you enter."

"In the early hours of this morning, some boys coming into town, mentioned a gory accident they had seen on the outskirts of Kaseh. The bus had run into a van, leaving no survivors."

Mr. Laskana asked the boys if they could remember the plate number of the bus. They could; it was the same bus you and the lady…"

The sand swayed to meet me. The earth became pestilent. The sun blazed with loss and shrouds. Someone poured a bucket of cold water on me. The water invaded my being. A rude awakening. Chili pepper in my raw wounds. O, I would have listened to a thousand sermons just to hear her voice again. Another torrent of water poured on me. I opened my eyes, irritated, willing the storm to stop. And my eyes beheld Crystal. She was smiling. She was unruffled. She was waking me up with clear water.

Boxer Shorts

"Go to the third floor, walk to the end of the corridor. At the end of the corridor, turn left. You will see three offices. The office of the man you are looking for is in the middle and he will leave at twelve noon to catch his school run. You have just five minutes, so beat it…"

I throw the kind man my thanks and hit the stairs, talking three at a leap… if only my mother could see me now. The daughter who was always the last to get out of bed racing as if time was gong bankrupt. I made it at the dot of twelve and I am confronted by the lecturer slamming his door with an excuse as old as fire.

"Excuse me, sir, could you kindly sign my tutorial card?"

I ask pleadingly, panting and looking suitably sober.

"Young lady, you had all morning. I am on my way out now. And I wont be back, see me tomorrow."

He turns on his heels and strides out. My shoulders slump. Did he think I had been playing games all day? Would two seconds really alter his day? I am at the end of my tether, ready to be unladylike. I ache to sit right on the corridor. I am swaying like palm trees strung right through with tiny birds' nests.

Nobody warned me that the university orientation week would be this complicated. For four hours I had been running around town, filing court affidavits, swearing and counter swearing to be on my best behaviour for the next four years.

I had gone through the rigours of a full medical examination and was still registering for my departmental courses and filling tutorial cards. I lean against the wall. Weariness washes all over me and I close my eyes…

"It is unhealthy to fall asleep on your feet."

I open my eyes and it is my friend the pathfinder, the man who gave me directions a few minutes earlier.

"Were you lucky? Did he sign your cards?"

"No, the man is just plain insensitive."

"Well, you had better get used to him if you are going to be in his class, he is a sticker for punctuality. You look ready to drop. Where are you staying? I'd like to give you a ride."

"Saminaka Hall."

I fall into step beside him. I sleepily stumble on the stairs, he firmly grips my hand,

"...Easy, I will soon have you in bed."

I survive the stairs and we walk to his car. It's a battered Suzuku Sidekick jeep with the sun roof down.

"I think we should get properly introduced before you fall asleep in my arms." I wake up very quickly, in time to catch his name.

"I am Ocha Amadi, I am a human rights activist. I run the local corps of Rights Africa."

For the first time I really look at him. He is tall with high cheek bones. Coffee coloured, he has long slim fingers. His shirt is open at the neck and tucked into khaki trousers. His feet are sheltered in loafers. His eyes are red, the red of the setting sun.

"Call me Dolapo. My surname is Elias. It is obvious that I am a brand new undergraduate and your red eyes tell me you need to catch up on some overdue sleep."

"Yeah, I've been up all night, distributing some flyers all over campus."

We get into his car and he starts tearing down the road.

"Easy, don't break the speed limit."

"I like to drive fast, that way, any car trailing me will be forced to reveal itself."

"Are you James Bond?"

"I deal in sensitive information. I have to watch my back all the time."

"So what kind of flyers were you distributing?"

"Well, just a couple of messages to sensitise the people. Our people are too complacent. They easily accept bad leadership.

They need to be woken up… we could use a smart young woman like you."

"Well, I'll see."

He drives into the parking lot of Saminaka Hall and I get out. He scribbles his address hurriedly and hands it over to me.

"Pretty woman, do come to see me soon." I murmur my thanks as he drives away.

Twenty-one days later, on my way back from a boring chemistry class, I see Ocha standing in front of the ground nut seller at the faculty car park and smiling at me. I walk up to him and he takes my hands, pouring some groundnuts into them.

"You completely abandoned me."

"No, you know how it is. I have had to settle down to my lectures. I am just coming from a class and I am starving."

"So why don't we hop to my house for a quick lunch?"

"I hope the lunch won't be your own cooking."

"You would be surprised. I almost won a zonal cooking competition two years ago."

"Alright, I will taste and see."

We drive off and stop in front of a bungalow nestled among the trees on street four of the university staff quarters.

"How come you have a university staff house?"

"I don't own the house, I'm a tenant and I live with my friend who is a university lecturer."

He opens the door and invites me to make myself comfortable. I take him at his word and ask to use the bathroom. It is painted powder pink. As I sit on the toilet, my eyes are drawn to an army of satin panties in different colours – blue, black, red, green, aquamarine, turquoise, pink, all strung up on a home dryer. They are beautiful, exquisitely designed like creations straight out of the Victoria Secret catalogue.

I flush the toilet and leave in time to see Ocha sitting at the table.

"The ladies of the house must be…"

"There are no ladies of the house."

"So who owns the panties collection in the bathroom?"

"They are mine."

I am incredulous. "You wear Satin Panties!"

"Why are you looking so shocked? I call them my boxer shorts. They feel very comfortable, very luxurious, almost as if I have nothing on. Don't look at me that way. Sit down. Food is ready."

I sit down with shaking legs, mentally noting the available doors. He comes near me and puts his hands on my shoulders.

"Hey! Relax..Your shoulders are so tense."

"I'm cool, I'm okay."

"Alright… you attracted me the first day I saw you.

I had this very strong urge to kiss you. Something told me you and I would go places."

"Please, take your hands off me."

I try to remove his hands but his grip is too strong.

"Relax baby, I feel like a woman right now. And you are here. I feel like you. Why don't you relax and let us groove together?"

"Ocha. take your hands off me. I don't want you. Can't you respect my right to be left alone?"

"Come on I feel like a woman. I'm not a monk…"

I kick my heels like a crazy man, wondering how I ever walked into this mess. I am suddenly aware of the brutal intensity of the noonday sun in the house of Mr. Ocha Amadi, the human rights activist, co-ordinator of Rights Africa, who feels like a woman. I relax and try to smile. I succeed in catching him off guard for a few seconds. I swivel on my heels, duck under his arm and head for the nearest door. I grab the door handle, pull it forcefully. It is locked. The fool! He must have locked it when I went to the toilet. As I move to see it if I can kick the door open, he pulls my feet from behind. I land on my face. Blood spills from my mouth. I scream and try to get up. He slaps me hard. I spit in his face and try to turn on my side but he pins me down with an arm and a leg. He unzips his trousers. He is wearing white satin panties.

Poised on the axle of this second, I know I must prevail or perish. No, I will not go under gently. My father's voice rings in my memory, "You can't lose, if you don't quit." Like a drowning swimmer makes one final grip on life, I unleash every reservoir of strength in me. My reflexes are all awake. I rear up suddenly and scratch his face with all the energy in my nails. I kick his groin with the fury of a defeated gold medallist who must now fight for the bronze. No, I will not go down gently. He lets out a primordial scream. Like the flying cork of a champagne bottle, I jump to my feet. I do not stop to look. l race to the other door, battering it with much desperation and all the prayers l could summon. The door splinters open. Bruised and bleeding, urinating on myself, I seize the open path.

Sister

Those legs just had to be hers. The billowing skirt too. Standing where the staircase turns sharply into the outer arena and waiting for the poet, I see her legs. Striding, she comes into complete view, the familiar sash, the always-present headband, eyes ever so ready to dare. Slowly, I melt into her hug.

"Folu." She gets my name wrong and I do not try to correct her. "When did you come?"

"Just a few minutes ago," I tell her. "Say, you are looking good. Bright smile and all."

I tell her I have come to chase the poet for an interview.

"You know, how he manages to pick up poetry from the grass at his feet and all that. I might not stay the night though, unless there is a blue moon spectacular enough to grip me."

We soon go our separate ways, planning to meet again in three hours time.

Meanwhile I see the poet. We talk and again, I am struck by his gift for speech, his capacity to exude the freshness for the word so much so that new things happen to his listeners. Trying to net him into a controversial corner, I ask,

"What by your own judgement should be the thematic core of the serious word?"

He laughs and I feel small.

"The word cannot be bound like a cluster of broom sticks. It heaves like the sea. A man writes a word, the word looms larger than him. I say, let all be written. Love stories, thriller, all poetry, all drama. Let the words flow."

Smart guy! Real slippery smart. I probe further, "Let all be written, will you write all?"

"By writing all, I am not saying life or craft should be thrown into the trash can. I mean let us aesthetically speak for the truth of our world."

He smiles and his smile makes him look mischievous in a vulnerable baby sense. I search his eyes, hoping to find revealed in them some major news angle. I find no such treasure and I get ready to leave. Why not rehearse my minimum French?

"*Au Revoir*, Mr. Poet. Merci, thanks for the time we have spent talking."

"You are welcome, young lady," as if he were much older than I...

I step into the shadeless sun and laugh as I remember an Irish acquaintance of mine scratching his arm and peeling from the heat of a nonchalant Lagos noon. It was a sight at once piteous and funny. As I walk towards her hall, the university's sights bloom before and around me. I spot a students' carnival; their queen, naïve, fearfully rides a horse.

I soon get to her hall. I step into the corridor leading to her room. What her room number is, I do not remember. I walk slowly, peeping into room after room through the open doors and windows. Perhaps, l will see her face through one of the open windows. I reach the end of the corridor, only failure. I turn back. At the middle of the corridor, I make bold to enter the room on my left to ask of her. As I knock, it is her voice I hear beckoning me in. I walk in and do not say I missed my way. I brightly smile.

"Hi, back from your lecture?"

"Yes, sit down. How did the interview go?"

"Fine, I got some material to delight my editor and earn me my overdue leave."

"You look wearied out, let me get you a cold coke. You can't beat the feeling, you know."

"My dear, a glass of ice-cold water beats coke hands down any day. Just get me some cold water."

She has no refrigerator and she goes out to get the water. From where, I do not ask. I look around her walls. Nothing is new. I see she is still keeping her old birthday cards. Books, a bible, perfume and those other ingredients that help make a woman lie around in compact disorder. Her room looks like home, lived in. Pots tucked under the bed, slippers peeping from under her armchair. I move to the table and see an unfinished poem and I skim through the opening lines:

"Hug me
in the dazzling sunlight
to the chorus of morning birds…"

I smile. Sola! She comes in with the water. Gratefully, I gulp it, then mischievously ask, "writing a poem for a new love?"

She responds shyly. "Sorting out myself, you might say, and Fola, (this time she gets my name right), you cannot leave today. There are some new poems of mine I would like you to see, and I know it's no use letting you take them back to Lagos. You would be too busy there to look at them. So now you are here, I ain't gonna let you go."

"All right." I give in quite readily. "Traveling back to Lagos in this hot sun is not an attractive prospect. Besides, I am not needed in the office till tomorrow afternoon." She smiles happily and I continue, "I might as well use the opportunity to search for a nail file in the university shopping complex. Would you like to come along?" She nods and slips on her sneakers.

* * *

We get to the shopping complex and I find the nail file in the first shop we enter. It is selling for N7.50 but I am hungry for window-shopping. I turn to her, "why not let us look in some other stores? We might find it cheaper."

She agrees. We leave and enter the next shop where it is selling for N6.

"Nigeria", I exclaim, "just the next shop and there is already a N1.50 difference."

I pick the nail file and almost move to pay for it but I feel in my bones that somewhere, among the shops still ahead, I will get it cheaper. I drop it and we look around the shop instead. I caress designer perfumes. Chloe, Anaïs Anaïs, alas, I'm too poor to buy any. With a regretful sigh, I pull her by the hand

and we leave for the next shop. Looking in through the glass are three little boys gazing desirously at the displayed toys. One of them is carrying a bottle that draws my attention, I look closer. It is a mini aquarium!

"Son, is this aquarium for sale?

"It is," he replies, "for ten naira"

I take the bottle from his hands and look close. Inside five little fishes are having a ball over little rocks. My office desk would appreciate their presence. I tell the boy,

"Son, take eight naira!"

"All right," he says.

"How about six naira?"

"No, auntie! Remember I am selling it with the bottle and bottles are expensive, you know."

I insist, "I will pay six naira."

"All right!" He accepts and I give him the money.

Sola and I gaze admiringly at the little fish, lost in their natural charm. A man passes by us and mutters under his breath, "Silly women!" We laugh with each other and enter the shop. We find the nail file and it is for N4.50. This time, I buy it and we retrace our steps towards the university gate. It was getting to night. The early moon was already up, stars too. On the other side of the road, a night market was gathering. Clutching the aquarium, I look in Sola's eyes, they have turned wistful. She soon speaks.

"I am longing for roasted corn and a stroll through the night market. Let us go. I will help carry the aquarium."

The plea in her eyes is too intense. Moreover, the idea of strolling through a night market, chewing roasted corn and lugging an aquarium sounds like fun. Besides, I need some crayfish for fish food. I turn with her and cross the road into the night market. We stroll on, till we meet a little girl roasting corn over an open charcoal fire. We stop and ask the price. It's fifty kobo each.

"Are you sure it's fresh?" Sola presses...

"Aa, auntie," she quickly replies, "my corn is very fresh. My elder brother just harvested them from our farm this morning. Taste this small one. You will see I am right."

We taste it. It seems fresh but we are not quite sure. We choose two corn cobs and ask her to roast them for us. Sola sees a log, lying a few yards away. We go to sit on it and the sights and sounds of night close upon us. The moon, full like a fulfilled vow, shimmers in silence. Oil lamps lighting the market are like fireflies in the night forest. People haggle. Two dogs howl at each other. A baby cries. The little girl brings our prickly hot corns. Sola reaches for hers with an eagerness so ready to conquer. She laughs, a musical laughter as she puts the corn to her lips like a flute, her teeth clinging to it like a trumpeter to his trumpet and I look her full in the eyes. As l look her full in the eyes, it dawns upon me quite simply that I love her.

Obinna the Vulture

A shower of stones will soon land on the roof. The stones will slide off the roof…patter, patter like a family of insolent Lagos rats defying rat-traps and mouse poison. The stones will land on the ground, bouncing off the hard concrete. They will skid to a stop at the feet of his assistants. Once again, the street traders will gather and wonder, speculating with tired voices, pointing their fingers at the spectacle on his roof.

He will scream at his servant,

"You lazy bones! Can't you drive it off? Take heavier stones. Get a catapult…Sling some shots at it. Get it off!"

And Okon will reply,

"But Oga, we have tried our best, it keeps coming back. I think we should get a dane gun and shoot it down."

Startled, he will turn to Okon,

"Make sure you don't use a gun on it. Drive it with stones. Do you understand?"

Okon will nod his head, muttering under his breath. He will probably curse his boss. The assembled on-lookers will present their opinions.

"Oga, it is best to shoot it down. The stones are not working. It keeps coming back".

"Mr. Ogbonna, it is best to bring it down with a bullet. It has been rather persistent. Its behaviour is very unusual. Perhaps your enemies sent it to harass you."

"Oga, why you no wan shoot am?"

He will ignore their snide remarks and derisive laughter. He will retire to the haven that is his bedroom.

* * *

This hour of reckoning unsettles him. And there is no escape route. The tightrope has cut in mid stream. Where is his hiding place? The vulture on his roof will not let go. It cannot be vanquished with stones. It transverses his dreams. Bird of carrion. Carnivorous. Its blood red beak fresh from the carcass. The beady eyes mock him, "You know you cannot kill me and live," they say, taunting him. "Once upon a time, before you became a man again, you were a vulture…"

* * *

It says the truth. It lies not. Once upon a time, he was a vulture. He had woken up four mornings before that time, living in want. His house rent had expired. He was condemned to incessant harassment by the housing agent. His girlfriend was pregnant and he could not even afford money for her ante-natal clinic. His kid brother had sent him a note, the day before, asking for school fees. He woke up that morning, longing for any deliverance from the avalanche of lack in his life. Without troubling to clean his mouth or take a bath, he wore his shoes, threw on a shirt over his faithful, everlasting pair of jeans and hurried out of his little room. He went to seek the wisdom of his friend, Ejike, who had suddenly acquired wealth over-night. A proverb says, 'if you keep quiet, your troubles will also keep quiet. No one will know where the pinch is in your shoes. You will not be offered a messiah.' He would tell Ejike his troubles. Surely, Ejike would be willing to help.

Ejike's shop was already open when he got there. A large shop halved into two rooms with a plywood partition across the breadth of the shop. The front room smelt of grease and engine-oil like a motor-mechanic's workshop. Ejike was a vehicle spare-parts dealer for Toyota, Peugeot and Honda cars. He stocked new and 'fairly-used' automobile parts. The second room was his office and relaxation room. Ejike hailed him as he entered the shop.

"Ogbonna! Ogbonna! Ogbonna!"

"Yes! That is my name!"

"Cunning man die, cunning man bury am."

"All is correct."

"Welcome my friend. Come inside. You are the true son of your father. Obinna and I were just discussing you, come in, come in…"

Ejike ushered Ogbonna into the inner room. Obinna leapt up from his chair as soon as he saw his friend.

"Ogbonna! The lion of his father's house. Welcome! You are the true son of your father. I was just telling Ejike how both of us were drowning our sorrows over bowls of palmwine last night. Ha, my friend, life is indeed hard. I came to see Ejike this morning for help. At Christmas, what will I tell my people back home? Will I return empty handed, when young men old enough to be my kid brothers come home to take chieftancy titles with their new BMW cars?"

"My brother, may we not return home empty handed. May we not become carriers of slippers for our age-mates."

The three men chorused "Amen."

"Ejike, our friend, we have come. A bush rat does not run in the afternoon if there is nothing chasing it. Ejike, you know our troubles. Be our path finder, help us to find a way out of the maze of poverty."

Ejike noisily cleared his throat and swallowed the phlegm.

"My brothers. You have spoken. I have heard you. Our people say, he who eats alone, dies alone. Food is sweeter when you eat with your friends. May we never eat alone. It is true that life is now hard in Nigeria. Even rich people have their problems. May our troubles not lack a solution."

Obinna and Ogbonna said, "Amen!"

"My brothers, at a time like this, it takes a man of courage to find good money. You cannot pluck naira from the trees. You need to look for it. In the days when I was poor, I was poorer than the street dogs. They could at least roam the rubbish dumps and find something to eat. I knew the bite of hunger. I lost so much weight, people were begging me to stop fasting.

I was not on a fast. It was hunger. I decided to go consult one-eyed Egbunike, companion-of-the-gods. My brothers, do I have your ears?"

"We are listening."

"Egbunike gave me a fearsome assignment. Only men of steel can do it. I must ask you, Are you men enough? Can you stare death in the face and not run?"

"We are men."

Obinna continued, "Ejike, do you not remember my grandfather, killer of elephants who rescued the seven villages of Idohana from the trampling feet of the ivory-husked one? And my father, toast of the village maidens' songs, reputed for his bravery and courage? I come from a long line of strong men. What is this assignment? I shall do it and more."

"My friends, you have spoken like men but I cannot tell you the assignment. I can only take you to the one-eyed one. Come back in another two days. I shall take you to Egbunike."

* * *

Ejike kept his word. He took his friends to Egbunike, a wizened old medicine man who lived in two rooms at Amukoko. The signboard outside his home read:
EGBUNIKE, THE ONE-EYED ONE.
COMPANION-OF-THE-GODS.
TRADITIONAL MEDICINE EXPERT.
For all your horoscope, star-gazing, astrology and palmistry.
Get the right medicine for Love, money, success, power and sex.
I cure impotency, barrenness, gonorrhea, syphilis, watery sperm and premature ejaculation.
I protect you from all your enemies.

As soon as they sat on the goat skin spread out in front of him, Egbunike said to them,

"My sons, welcome. Poverty is a bad thing but you have come to the right place."

Ogbonna and Obinna looked at each other amazed.

Ejike told them, "Papa knows everything."

"Not everything my son, only what the gods tell me. My sons, you are welcome. The path to wealth is a torturous road. Many men set out on it and never arrive. Only strong men survive. Do you have a strong heart?"

"Papa, poverty is a disease. We are strong men. We will do whatever you ask of us."

"Alright, listen carefully. The medicine I will give you is a very simple one. I will give you my special 'creative' juice. At one in the night, in pitch darkness on a crossroad of four paths, you will mix the juice with one shot of liqueur. You shall drink it in one gulp. After about five minutes, you will begin to grow feathers. You will become a vulture."

"Papa!"

"Be quiet, child. Let me finish!"

"You will fly from that spot and look for the nearest place where there has been an accident involving human beings. You will eat human flesh. After your meal, you will fly back directly to me. I shall give you an 'antidote' drink and you will return to your normal human selves."

Obinna ran outside, retching and vomiting. Ogbonna said, "Papa, I am a man. I'll do it..." Ogbonna left the one-eyed one with the juice safely in his hands. It was greyish coloured like a corpse kept in ice.

* * *

At 1:05 am, in the night of a new day, Ogbonna became a vulture. Flying over the sleeping residents in crowded Lagos houses, he began to hunger for blood. The lights of the city twinkled beneath him. The swamp flowers of the Lagos lagoon sent up a sour-sweet aroma. He heard the resonance of drunken voices, the dare-devilry incited by alcohol when sloshed men think that the yawning chasm before them is a tarred road, awaiting their footsteps. And he shook his head at them all. For lesser mortals did not know the power he now had. The power to eat their flesh. To suck their blood. "Beware!" he screamed, "hide from my paths or you will become my meal."

His carrion instinct led him to a fresh accident at Oworonsoki. An over-speeding car had crashed into a stationary truck packed by a couldn't-care-less owner in the middle of the road. The driver had died instantly, his blood dripping, dripping, congealing on the lonely road. Ogbonna tucked into the corpse, savouring the fat of the liver, slowly flapping his wings in wonderment of human flesh. He flew back to Egbunike after his meal. Egbunike had a thick creamy soup waiting for him in a bowl. Perched on a wooden stool in front of Egbunike, Ogbonna was given seven and a half spoonfuls of the antidote soup. In five minutes, his human body began to emerge. First, his legs shot out. Then his arms and his head. And his trunk. The vulture's feathers fell off him and lay scattered on the floor.

Egbunike chuckled, his nearly toothless gums gave off a reddish glow in the lantern light.

"Welcome back into your human flesh. Did you enjoy your meal?"

Ogbonna stuttered and could say nothing coherent. He still felt as if he was in a dream.

Egbunike continued, "Here, take this pot. Gather all the vulture's feathers on the floor into a pot. Cover it tightly. Keep it in a private room. No woman in her menstrual period must be permitted to enter. Open the pot every morning. You will find crisp wads of five hundred naira notes. You can now go…"

Ogbonna walked out, befuddled and dazed. He rode a borrowed bicycle home through the quiet streets and installed the pot under his bed. He climbed into bed and promptly fell asleep. Waking up the next morning, he hurriedly drew out the pot under the bed. He opened it. It was filled with fresh naira notes...

Obinna, seeing Ogbonna's new found wealth gathered his courage and went back to Egbunike. Egbunike gave him the 'Money' drink. He too became a vulture and had his fill of human carrion. On his flight back to Egbunike, he heard a woman's wailing, renting the night with her lament. He flew nearer and nearer. The lament was coming from Egbunike's home. His daughter was rolling on the floor, refusing to be consoled.

"My father, Egbunike, why have you left me fatherless? O companion-of-the-gods, why did you die?"

Obinna fell from the sky in shock and landed with a thud in Egbunike's courtyard.

No one noticed the vulture in the sorrow of the night...

Obinna's family raised a search party and declared him missing to the police. Advertisements carrying his photograph, name, age, height, and date of birth were published in the national newspapers and announced on television. His friends, Ejike and Ogbonna, went to look for him at Egbunike's home. They found that the gods had taken the one-eyed one. And he had not passed on the secrets of his 'money making' drink and its 'soup antidote' to his assistants...

In the days after, Obinna the vulture began his mournful vigil, standing sentry on Ogbonna's roof.

*9 7 8 1 8 5 6 5 7 1 1 0 4 *